*Stories of Resilience
and Courage*

Stories of Resilience and Courage

Women Coaches Form a Global Community

Sheila Hurtig Robertson

IGUANA

Copyright © 2023 Sheila Hurtig Roberston
Published by Iguana Books
720 Bathurst Street
Toronto, ON M5S 2R4

All rights reserved. No part of this publication may be reproduced, stored in a retrieval system or transmitted, in any form or by any means, electronic, mechanical, recording or otherwise (except brief passages for purposes of review) without the prior permission of the author.

Publisher: Cheryl Hawley
Editor: Paula Chiarcos
Front cover design: Jonathan Relph

ISBN 978-1-77180-672-5 (paperback)
ISBN 978-1-77180-671-8 (epub)

This is an original print edition of *Stories of Resilience and Courage*.

Dedication

To the intern coaches for your commitment, passion, humanity, and friendship:
Lini Kazim, Victoria Grant, Dumisani Chauke, Tina Hoeben, Laura Kerr Lewis, Mildred Gamba, Soraya Julaya Santos, Amanda Booth, Cordelia Norris, Carolyne Anyango Kola, Jill Perry, Bah Chui Mei, Isabelle Lindor-André, Martine Dugrenier, Endurance Ojokolo, Grace Mmolai, Amanda Murphy, Sheila Gakii, Mpho Madi, and Evangeline Collier.

To the mentors for your commitment to ensuring the Women Coach Internship Programme (WCIP) was a successful experience for your intern coaches:
Grant Robbins, Norma Plummer, Alan Cooke, Tonya Verbeek, John Odhiambo, Nalis Bigingo, Martyn Wilby, Peter Lau, Jackie Newton, John Anzrah, Patrick Sahajasein, the late Nico Coetzee, Zuraidi Puteh, Luza Lechedzani, Dale Stevenson, Steve Gladding, Olu Sule, Daniel Trépanier, Stu Ross, and Orlando Dingne.

To CGF Vice President (and my husband) Bruce Robertson, for the conception of the WCIP, for ensuring that it became reality, for your steadfast encouragement, and for inspiring me to go beyond what I think is possible. Neither the WCIP nor this book could have happened without you.

To Sheilagh Croxon, for exemplifying leadership and commitment in bringing the WCIP to life.

To CGF Director of Sport Ann-Louise Morgan, for providing wisdom and experience to the selection process.

Contents

Introduction	1
Chapter One: Lini Kazim, Malaysia	7
Chapter Two: Victoria Grant, New Zealand	19
Chapter Three: Dumisani Chauke, South Africa	30
Chapter Four: Tina Hoeben, Canada	40
Chapter Five: Laura Kerr Lewis, Northern Ireland	51
Chapter Six: Mildred Gamba, Uganda	63
Chapter Seven: Soraya Julaya Santos, Mozambique	74
Chapter Eight: Amanda Booth, England	85
Chapter Nine: Cordelia Norris, New Zealand	98
Chapter Ten: Carolyne Anyango, Kola Kenya	110
Chapter Eleven: Jill Perry, Canada	122
Chapter Twelve: Bah Chui Mei, Malaysia	134
Chapter Thirteen: Isabelle Lindor-André, Mauritius	146
Chapter Fourteen: Martine Dugrenier, Canada	158
Chapter Fifteen: Endurance Ojokolo, Nigeria	171
Chapter Sixteen: Grace Mmolai, Botswana	182
Chapter Seventeen: Amanda Murphy, New Zealand	193
Chapter Eighteen: Sheila Gakii, Kenya	203
Chapter Nineteen: Mpho Madi, South Africa	214

Chapter Twenty: Evangeline, Collier England 226

Appendix One: CGF Women Coach Internship Programme Application Form 237

Appendix Two: CGF Women Coach Internship Programme Guidelines 241

Appendix Three: Women Coach Internship Programme 243

Appendix Four: The WCIP Intern Coaches and Their Mentor Coaches 247

Introduction

The Women Coach Internship Programme (WCIP), launched by the Commonwealth Games Federation (CGF) at the 2018 Commonwealth Games in Gold Coast, Australia, was, according to the twenty women who participated, a resounding success, not least for the powerful and enduring bonds of friendship and support that resulted.

Some months before the Games, the seventy Commonwealth Games associations were asked to recommend women coaches who could benefit from the opportunity to "fill a specific and meaningful role within their country's coaching team and on the field of play."[1] (See Appendix One.)

The goal of the WCIP was to ensure that the intern coaches would be fully embedded within their teams, thereby guaranteeing a tangible international coaching experience that would augment their resumes. "Support would be provided by a carefully selected mentor, usually the relevant teams' head coach." In addition, the CGF would appoint a woman programme director "with a strong coaching background who would prepare an educational program for delivery throughout the Games"[2] and an experienced communications consultant to profile and promote the intern coaches.

---

[1] Sheila Hurtig Robertson, "WCIP Virtual Reunion: Unique Bonds Reinforced," *Commonwealth Sport*, April 19, 2020, https://www.commonwealthsport.com/news/3073789/wcip-virtual-reunion-unique-bonds-reinforced.

[2] Robertson, "WCIP Virtual Reunion."

Chosen to direct the WCIP was Sheilagh Croxon, a fierce champion and developer of women coaches and a three-time Canadian Olympic coach in the sport of artistic swimming. Her teams have been successful, earning medals at two Olympic Games and several World Championships. Sheilagh is sought-after worldwide as a coach, choreographer, and consultant. Given my years of writing about women coaches within the Canadian and Commonwealth systems, I volunteered to provide communications support.

And so it was that on April 5, 2018, twenty women coaches from every corner of the Commonwealth crowded into a small room in the Gold Coast Athletes Village for their first meeting. No one knew what to expect and there was no hint that something extraordinary was about to happen. But almost immediately, a powerful connection was established, which became, and remains, a key characteristic of this group.

The energy in the room was palpable — and quite surprising — since only Sheilagh and I knew each other. We'd been friends and colleagues for years and share common principles and perspectives, but neither of us anticipated the strong bonds that emerged so quickly. It was remarkable.

One fascinating aspect of the WCIP is the interns' diverse backgrounds and languages, which range from growing up in farming communities to small towns to sophisticated urban centres. Nevertheless, there was much common ground: all were athletes, all are committed to improving opportunities for girls to succeed in sport and in life, and all have a strong desire to give back to sport, which they acknowledge has given them so much.

Having been deeply involved with the WCIP from start to finish, Sheilagh Croxon is convinced of the importance of telling the stories written on these pages and also of the immense value of a WCIP experience to these interns and, indeed, to aspiring women coaches everywhere. "I feel extremely fortunate to have gotten to know each of the incredible women coaches featured in this book. Learning firsthand about each of their journeys was a life-altering experience for me. Their stories must be shared, not only because the barriers that they have faced and overcome are real and prevalent, but most importantly, because they are a source of inspiration, for other women coaches, for the next generation, and people of minority in any profession."

During a Zoom call a year after Gold Coast, I was challenged by the intern coaches and Sheilagh to tell their stories in a book. The challenge proved to be irresistible even though it took longer than expected to complete. Work commitments, COVID-19, telecommunication challenges, and other incidentals slowed but did not stop the process. Initial interviews were conducted throughout 2020, with follow-ups in 2021, 2022, and 2023.

Writing this book has been one of the most rewarding experiences of my professional life and, personally, it's an honour and a privilege to know all the wonderful people involved in the WCIP.

The Intern Coaches Reflect on the WCIP Experience

Lini Kazim, Malaysia: "I am excited to have the opportunity to experience a high-level race as a coach and hope to bring back the required skill and knowledge to coach Malaysian athletes at the national and international levels."

Victoria Grant, New Zealand: "Being immersed with our national team at a pinnacle event will be a great experience and will help me in future endeavours."

Dumisani Chauke, South Africa: "The WCIP means that the CGF takes women coaches seriously and has decided to play an influential and critical role in the empowerment and uplifting of women coaches."

Tina Hoeben, Canada: "It is a great opportunity and one that I am very excited to participate in."

Laura Kerr Lewis, Northern Ireland: "This is an innovative programme and I very much appreciate that this is a central part of the CGF's Gender Equality Strategy."

Mildred Gamba, Uganda: "It means the world to me to be given the opportunity to be part of the WCIP. Every experience was memorable ... WCIP personnel [are] very accessible and lovely and supportive."

Soraya Julaya Santos, Mozambique: "The WCIP gave me tools to gain confidence in myself as a coach and as a person, sharing my point of view, and having better communication with my athletes. After Gold Coast, my club won the National Championship, and my National Olympic Committee involved me in national team selection."

Amanda Booth, England: "It is fantastic to be given this opportunity to work with the senior swimmers. I am very grateful and proud to be selected. My most memorable experience was listening to the presentations by the intern coaches at the WCIP reception. Mildred (Gamba) was inspirational and moving and the WCIP personnel were very supportive and encouraging."

Cordelia Norris, New Zealand: "I loved all of it ... It was one of the most amazing things I've ever taken part in. My learnings include self-awareness from the Myers-Briggs assessment; insight into different sports and learning about challenges people face internationally and how they overcome them; that there are other ways of learning other than traditional university or college; don't try to be a male coach because female coaches bring something special to the table; and the importance of team culture."

Carolyne Anyango Kola, Kenya: "The WCIP is important ... as a woman being granted a chance to interact with fellow women coaches and build networks so we can help each other in understanding how to best coach our athletes."

Jill Perry, Canada: "The CGF's investment in this programme is validation that women coaches matter and is acknowledgement that gender equality issues need to be addressed. It was important to come together every morning to share and recharge our collective energies and commitment to the process of moving women forwards in sport."

Bah Chui Mei, Malaysia: "I am honoured to be selected as it gives me a chance to do what I have dreamt of, which is to initiate a proper programme for women in coaching ... I had two role models instead of one, and I really admired Sheilagh and Sheila for their incredible and wonderful actions to gather us all from different countries to share one vision: to be a high-performance coach and a daring one."

Isabelle Lindor-André, Mauritius: "Mentoring is crucial to my career ... A big thank-you to Sheilagh and Sheila for their work and devotion to empower women coaches."

Martine Dugrenier, Canada: "I decided on a coaching career to give back to the next generation, to help athletes achieve their dreams, and to help them achieve their potential in wrestling."

Endurance Ojokolo, Nigeria: "The most valuable thing I learned from the WCIP was how to build up my self-confidence, which helped me to believe in myself a lot more, especially in my ability to make changes and decisions to benefit my athletes and make a difference in my sport. I now see myself as a woman coach who can produce the same results, and even better, as other coaches. I can confidently say that I am outspoken and understand the key roles to being an effective coach ... I knew my work [in Gold Coast] would speak for me and that's exactly what happened."

Grace Mmolai, Botswana: "Every day was memorable because sitting among women coaches with similar experiences enriched my spirit of confidence and self-belief in the coaching field ... I expect it [the WCIP] to bring attention to countries that are lagging behind in terms of female empowerment."

Amanda Murphy, New Zealand: "[The WCIP] ... will prepare me for future coaching opportunities at this level and give me a chance to connect with other women coaches at the same stage as me and from multiple sports and countries."

Sheila Gakii, Kenya: "Mentoring ... provides an avenue that allows me to interact and socialise with professionals and will facilitate success for me and for the development of badminton."

Mpho Madi, South Africa: "I love this initiative. Meeting all the incredible coaches from eleven countries and different sporting backgrounds but all with one goal: becoming the best coaches for our athletes. Because of the WCIP, women in coaching will grow because whatever I learn I will share with my fellow women coaches in my country and Africa as a whole."

Evangeline (Evie) Collier, England: "The WCIP has been one of the most rewarding and value-gaining experiences of my life. The support has been amazing, and the effectiveness of the support/knowledge has given me a new outlook to coaching."

The author, Sheila Hurtig Robertson, has an exit interview with Mildred Gamba of Uganda at the WCIP Reception.
Photo by Sheilagh Croxon

Chapter One

Lini Kazim

Malaysia

Nik Lini Hayati Nik Kazim's life journey has taken her far from Kota Bharu, Malaysia, where she was born on October 23, 1969. Near the border with Thailand, the town is the capital and royal seat of the state of Kelantan. One of four children close in age — Lini has two brothers, Harry and Rudi, and one sister named Roza — she describes a childhood in which sport was a huge part of daily life.

Lini calls her mother, Norma, the "tiger in the house. She would cook for us but would whip us all up when we were up to no good! She was active in sports, particularly badminton, until middle age."

Her father, Nik, was a physical education teacher and naturally encouraged his children to be active. "We were always running, climbing, kicking balls, cycling; there was never a moment when we weren't doing something physical. I remember going to school in the morning, throwing down my bag when I came home, and then I would be out until seven p.m. I only came home to have dinner and go to sleep."

Lini could have been a top-level competitor in any number of sports had such a pathway been encouraged, but despite the paternal insistence on physical activity, hers was a family where the expected careers were medicine or law, not sport. "Go outside, have fun, and that was about it."

In 1982, when she was twelve years old, Lini's parents sent her 500 kilometres away to attend Tunku Kurshiah College, located in Seremban, the capital of Negeri Sembilan, and one of the best all-girls residential schools under the aegis of Sekolah Berasrama Penuh, a school system established to nurture outstanding students.

The first three months away from her close-knit family were difficult for the lonely youngster. Compounding the situation were communication challenges. Kelantan Malay, the dialect spoken in Kota Bharu, differs from Bahasa Malaysia, the national language of Malaysia. Still, Lini understood the importance of the boarding school opportunity, not least for learning a second language. "When I was growing up, boarding school was the ultimate symbol of academic excellence, and so every parent wanted to send their kids to such an institution." Her siblings went to boarding schools and later pursued degree courses overseas: Harry in the United States, Roza in Ireland, and Rudi and Lini in England.

Upon graduation from secondary school in 1987, Lini was awarded a scholarship to study for her A-Levels (Advanced Levels) in physics, mathematics, and economics at Headington School in Oxford, England. Once again traumatised by a language barrier, she said: "I'm laughing now, but at the time it wasn't funny … I never wanted to open my mouth because I was so worried about pronouncing a word wrongly and using the wrong word."

Lini did well enough to be admitted to the University of Nottingham in 1989, graduating in 1992 with a law degree and then working in London for the next two years. Her grandfather, Ghazally, urged her to return to Malaysia, which was enjoying a boom in infrastructure development, and she heeded his advice.

Returning in 1994, Lini began her professional career as a legal consultant with the Canadian transportation company, SNC-Lavalin. Seconded to Bombardier, another Canadian company known as a global leader in aviation, she was involved in the procurement of Light Rail Transit (LRT) systems in Kuala Lumpur (KL) and Vancouver, British Columbia.

During her time with SNC-Lavalin, Lini met Montréal-born Franco Rende, a first-generation Québécois of Italian descent who was and remains an SNC-Lavalin employee in KL. The two met in the firm's KL office while working on the city's LRT system.

The two married on April 4, 1998, a date chosen because it fell on a Friday, which Lini hoped would be easy to remember as she is "hopeless" with dates. Their daughter, Natasha, was born on May 26, 2000, in KL, Lini returning from Vancouver at the end of 1999 to give birth. She then spent the next fourteen years working full time as a contract and procurement specialist in the oil and gas industry on projects for Chevron and Shell that took her throughout Asia, Europe, and Africa. For seven of those years, studying part time, she earned a master's of business administration through Heriot-Watt University, a public research institution based in Edinburgh, Scotland, graduating in 2006. Natasha travelled with Lini until she was ten years old. She was then sent to boarding school to ensure that her education wasn't disrupted.

Everywhere Lini went, she spent her weekends competing as a runner. Over the years, she built a solid reputation as a master's racer. When she hit a plateau, cross-training was suggested, and she opted for cycling to strengthen her muscles. This led to duathlon competitions with swimming as a recovery tool. "It was complete cross-training, and that is how I began triathlon in 2011." Results came quickly, culminating in her stellar performance at the 2014

IRONMAN Malaysia at Pulau Langkawi, where she was the fastest Malaysian woman in a gruelling event that consists of a 3.8-kilometre swim, a 180-kilometre cycle, and a 42.2-kilometre run, all this at the age of forty-five.

Lini Kazim

A Coaching Journey Begins

Following Langkawi, in a move that had long been in the works, Lini stepped away from law to concentrate on fulfilling her dream of pursuing her passion for sports, not necessarily as an elite athlete but as a coach. Her goal was to help make a difference in the lives of young people by giving them opportunities she didn't have when she was growing up.

Triathlon had first gained recognition in Malaysia following its Olympic debut at the 2000 Sydney Games. Steve Lumley, one of the world's most accomplished triathlon coaches, pioneered the sport in Malaysia and eventually became Lini's coach. After her success at Langkawi, her social media was flooded with messages from young triathletes asking for advice about training programmes and nutrition, and she grew excited by the prospect of developing young triathletes: "The need to correctly answer each individual's questions was the trigger to strengthen my decision to be a coach."

Lini gladly shared her experience, acquired Level 1 accreditation through the New Zealand Triathlon Association, and helped Lumley to establish a youth/junior development programme. "We got buzzed about triathlon; we had good swimmers, good cyclists, good runners; we just had to put them together ... It was so rewarding to have the youth bloom into junior elites under proper guidance, and that inspired me to continue Steve's good work after he returned to the United Kingdom ... Coaching gave me the chance for achievement with the young athletes. I wouldn't say that's living my life through the athletes, but it's trying to materialise for them the dream I had but [that] never happened."

Before long, Lini's aptitude for coaching was recognised by the Triathlon Association of Malaysia, which encouraged her to pursue higher-level coaching and expanded her experience by sending her to a training camp facilitated by world-class coaches from all over Asia. She also added an advanced diploma in nutrition to her credits. In 2016, she became head coach of Team TIME Triathlon (TTT), which is privately sponsored by TIME, a giant communications company in Malaysia. Guided by Lini, TTT grooms elite athletes to compete at major Games, such as the Southeast Asian Games, continental and World Championships, and the Commonwealth Games. The team's ultimate goal is participation at the 2028 Olympic Games.

WCIP Provides Significant Learnings

At the urging of the Olympic Council of Malaysia, Lini applied to participate in the Women Coach Internship Programme to be held during the 2018 Commonwealth Games in Gold Coast, Australia. She arrived there expecting the technical components of the programme to be the most relevant to her coaching development. To her surprise, from the first session, the WCIP was an eye-opener that sharply changed Lini's perspective. "I came back from Gold Coast a different coach. Because I was relatively inexperienced, I initially ignored the 'soft skills' because I worried about getting the athletes' programmes right rather than building relationships with them. In fact, through the WCIP, the soft skills had a bigger impact on me than what I learned from the technical sessions at Griffith University. Now I spend less time writing a programme and more on conversations with my athletes and really listening to their answers.

"This was a very important outcome because now the dynamics of our relationships are dramatically different. I can feel the trust they have in me, and the trust their parents have, and that is so important in building the relationship. It's not about running 400 metres in X minutes but about developing the motivation to do well."

A self-described theorist who enjoys delving into the many different coaching models, Lini summed up the WCIP as "a unique and exceptional learning experience."

As for her role as national team coach during the Games, Lini was assigned responsibility for the two Malaysian triathletes — Xian Hao Chong and Chen Yin Yang — by the National Sports Council of Malaysia. She understood that they viewed her appointment with trepidation. "When you're someone who hasn't been coaching for a long time, you sense they are questioning your ability to be there. I always had to prove to them that I had the appropriate qualifications. Of course, my mentor coach, Peter Lau, who was at the Games as a technical official, has much more experience, but these two are my athletes and so the council trusted me to take them through the Games."

The Gold Coast performance of Xian Hao Chong qualified him to compete at the 2018 Summer Youth Olympics in Buenos Aires, Argentina, with Lini selected to accompany him as national coach. She became a member of the coaching committee of the Malaysia Triathlon Association, providing a platform to ensure fair athlete selection for all major events and to develop inclusive programmes. Noteworthy, of the eleven athletes Malaysia sent to the 2019 Southeast Asia Games in the Philippines, half came from TTT.

Lini's goal is to ensure that her athletes will never say they didn't have a chance and will have no regrets. "I didn't have the opportunity to really excel in sports, so I try to create opportunities for them." Being able to build TTT reflects a recent societal shift in Malaysia.

"Having my athletes commit to the long term demonstrates a shift in the way our society views sport, and so does the support I get from their parents."

Lini has urged Malaysian universities to award scholarships so the triathletes can pursue excellence in education and in sport. "It's about having an impact on their lives in more ways than swim, cycle, and run. Triathlon is an expensive sport and is thought to be only for the privileged, but we have so much untapped talent and we must find the resources for them to excel. I must find a way to reach beyond those who come to me because they can afford the sport."

As a woman coach, Lini considers herself fortunate because the Malaysian triathlon community is welcoming but also because she produces successful athletes and she herself continues to excel competitively. A personal milestone came when she qualified to compete in the 50–54 age group at the 2020 IRONMAN 70.3 World Championship, postponed and then cancelled because of the COVID-19 pandemic. "Initially I was quite upset because I had a lot I wanted to accomplish for myself; having to push everything back two or three years is a long time when you're fifty years old."

Lini strives to be a role model for her athletes, as Lumley was for her. "For me, personally, racing is important, and I attribute my success to my athletes because they drive me to excel. I can't tell them to excel if I take it easy when competing … I'm not just dishing it out to them but am also living it by qualifying in my own capacity."

A Lesson in Adapting

The COVID-19 pandemic disrupted Lini's training and her coaching. Initially she concentrated on maintaining her fitness and varying her training regimen by participating in events such as the 2020 Perhentian Island Marathon Swim, in which two people take turns kayaking and swimming around an island in the middle of the sea. Competitors cover about sixteen kilometres around Pulau Besar, one of the coral fringed Perhentian Islands that lie off the northeastern coast of Malaysia in Terengganu State. She also took up mountain biking and, in typical Lini fashion, tackled a 200-kilometre ride through Malaysia, all to maintain her fitness level so she would be in competition form once Malaysia eased its COVID-related restrictions.

Keeping her athletes active and engaged was complicated by the cancellation of all races. Lacking a goal and coping with several total lockdowns, some experienced depression. Lini sympathised with their challenges because she herself endured a stressful one-month period during which restrictions confined her to her apartment. She communicated with her athletes every day using Skype or Zoom, presenting sessions covering topics relevant to their training, encouraging them to be open about what they were experiencing, and inviting nutritionists and psychologist to make presentations. A subsequent period of restricted lockdown, with everyone restrained within their own 10-kilometre radius, made coaching even more challenging. Lini said that nothing could replace physical coaching and being able to observe an athlete's breathing, tone, and mood, all of which affect performance. She noted with relief that, once the pandemic waned and the athletes could come together as a team, it wasn't long before their results returned to prepandemic levels.

Lini Kazim discusses tactics during a triathlon meet.

Always Learning, Always Travelling

A dedicated student of the art of coaching and committed to constant self-improvement, Lini has been mentored since 2017 by Ando Kenta, a Japanese coach who heads the Macau Triathlon Team. The two met at a triathlon training camp in Palenbang, Indonesia. "I was amazed at how much I didn't know after at observing him coach over that one week." Lini and Ando are in regular contact, meet at various races, and exchange ideas through email. The mentorship may be unofficial, but Lini consults him on virtually every aspect of triathlon.

In 2021, World Triathlon selected Lini for its how-to-mentor sessions, and she now mentors Lou Ann Ramos, a coach from the Philippines, through a programme that aims to increase and sustain the number of women and people with a disability in leadership roles in coaching, technical officiating, and governance in triathlon. "I wanted to be a mentor so I can be what Ando is to me, but the best part is that, even as a mentor, I learn a great deal from my mentee. I am a firm believer in mentoring, regardless of the side I am on."

Journeying Far and Wide

Lini's adventures are as awe-inspiring as they are wide ranging. In May 2022, she travelled to Kathmandu, Nepal, determined to reach Everest Base Camp (EBC), at the invitation of Ida Borhan, a friend from high school and an experienced hiker who arranged all the details of the adventure. "All I needed to do was say yes, and she took care of the rest."

The goal was to hike to EBC, but after passing the 4000-metre mark, with the air thinner and colder and the view only grey boulders, Lini started to develop a severe cough and could hardly breathe. She remembered getting up in the morning and panting, just trying to get out of bed. "Not wanting to jeopardise my health, I asked my guide to split the group so that Ida could continue to ascend to base camp while I descended to about 3,000 metres to get more oxygen. The descent was what was needed so that I could breathe again, but it wasn't sufficient for me to recover in time to attempt another ascent."

Despite falling ill and failing to reach EBC, Lini described the experience as her most memorable trip to date. "I love how simple life is in that part of the world. Even when it was so cold, even when the people had to use yak dung for fuel, even when they ate dhal rice every day, they were sufficiently happy. I realised that we just have way too much in life!"

In September 2021, accompanying her daughter Natasha to London, England, where the latter was studying for her bar examination, Lini ended up staying away from Malaysia for two months. During this time, she also visited friends in Munich and persuaded them to climb up to Neuschwanstein Castle in southwest Bavaria, Germany, even though they "hate exercise with a vengeance." Back in England, Lini was constantly on the move, catching up with Ida and visiting triathlon coach Lumley, friends from her A-Levels, an online Toastmasters friend, and a former work colleague. That is why, she explained, a three-week holiday stretched into two months.

Within Malaysia, Lini's travels usually coincide with various physically demanding activities. These include running a training camp for junior triathletes in Fraser's Hill, a resort area located in Pahang; swimming 6.5 kilometres across the South China Sea from Pulau Kapas to Marang, followed by a whale shark excursion in Tenggol Island; climbing to the summit of Mount Kinabalu, the country's highest mountain; blue water diving in Sipadan, considered one of the world's top diving destinations and the only oceanic island in Malaysia; cycling up Mount Jerai in Malaysia's highlands; and climbing and hiking in the Pyrenees before moving on to Bordeaux and Nantes.

For Lini, the singular moments are even more memorable than crossing a finish line. "In the swim across the sea, I vividly remember stopping at the 3.8-kilometre mark to chat with another competitor to make sure we were on the right path and learning how difficult it is to pee in a horizontal position! And even when coughing violently during the EBC trip, it was not the disappointment of failing to reach the base camp that enveloped my thoughts but the kindness of the people who took care of me, the serenity of the mountains — there is no noise pollution except for the occasional helicopter — and the natural beauty I had not experienced before."

Lini's destination choices are usually serendipitous. To celebrate their fiftieth birthdays, Lini and several friends opted for Morocco. "We listed a few countries and made our choice after considering certain factors: safety for female travellers, activities in which everyone could participate, a country which no one had visited, the length of the holiday, and cost."

Aside from London, Lini tends to avoid big cities. When she worked in the corporate world, her travels confined her to the four walls of an office, which could have been anywhere. She prefers mountains to a beach; walking, cycling, or train travel to driving. She isn't fazed by solo travel, books flexible travel dates, and shuns an agenda. "Every destination is exotic, and I always manage to find something fascinating about each place. The Eiffel Tower and the Empire State Building, for example, don't stir me as much as graffiti on walls or signboards. Favourites include 'Eyediology' for an optician's office, 'Band of Burgers' for a hamburger joint, and 'Duke of Uke' for a ukulele shop. I am quite easy to please!"

Most of Lini's adventures are solo. "Franco never stops me from pursuing my wildest dream, but neither does he encourage it. Natasha thinks I am a free-spirited individual who is constantly reading, learning, and travelling in search of a better me. She shares the same love of books and travel, so we spend many hours together exchanging opinions on past and future adventures."

In February 2023, World Triathlon certified Lini as a Level 2 coach. Candidates first spend two full calendar years on Level 1, enhancing "their capabilities by giving them sufficient breadth of knowledge ... to develop their future coaching knowledge and experience."[3]

---

[3] "Level 1 Coach Certification," World Triathlon, accessed September 19, 2023, https://www.triathlon.org/development/coach/level_1_coach_certification.

Most recently, Lini has been accepted into the latest edition of the Women in Sport High Performance Pathway (WISH)[4] starting in May 2023. It is a twenty-one-month programme organised by Olympic Solidarity and the University of Hertfordshire.

"I am truly excited!"

Note:

WCIP intern coach Martine Dugrenier completed WISH in 2022. See Chapter Fourteen.

WCIP intern coach Endurance Ojokolo is part of the 2024 cohort. See Chapter Fifteen.

---

[4] Women in Sport High Performance Pathway, Information for International Federations, 2022,
https://www.ibsf.org/images/news/Images/Summer_2022/Women_in_Sport_High_Performance/WISH_Information_for_International_Federations_004.pdf.

Chapter Two

Victoria Grant

New Zealand

Victoria Grant's childhood and teen years can best be described as peripatetic. Born in Auckland/Tāmaki Makaurau,[5] New Zealand, on August 26, 1982, to Robyn Blackledge and Ted Taiatini, who divorced when she was very young, Victoria attended nineteen primary and intermediate schools and three secondary schools during her first

---

[5] In New Zealand, the practice of giving locations two names began in the 1920s and became more common following the Treaty of Waitangi settlements in the 1990s and 2000s, as a way of honouring ancestral lands.

nineteen years. Making new friends only to quickly move on built her resilience and made her adept at adapting to change even as she acknowledged how difficult the lifestyle was.

Lacking roots meant not having a place to call her hometown, which Victoria described as "a sticking point." Near the end of her secondary school days, she found herself living in Putāruru on New Zealand's North Island for a longer than usual period; that small town became her "hometown." Despite the constant moving, she always excelled academically and was Māori Dux (the academic head of class) at Putāruru High School.

During these formative years, Victoria had little connection with her father, who was based in Auckland, mainly because the constant moves with her mother took her and her siblings, Nicole van der Wel and Katie and Joshua Blackledge, all over New Zealand. All that changed when, at the age of eighteen, she reconnected with Ted, who is a Māori, and her four half-siblings — Annie, Michelle, Margaret, and Mark Taiatini. Developing strong relationships with them changed her life. "I never had a close connection with [my father] — I always knew who he was but would only see him once a year at most — but I do now and that is why I feel strongly about family and *whenua*, an ancient Austronesian word meaning 'land.'"

Victoria's introduction to sport came as a seven-year-old and centred around netball, which she and her friends played at primary school. Gradually, her natural talent as a sprinter emerged and she raced during her secondary school years. At the age of eighteen, rugby entered her life almost by accident. "I was conned into a secondary school game when I was in seventh form. The team needed numbers to play a final. I knew nothing about rugby; all I knew was to do what they told me, which was to catch the ball on the wing and run as fast as I could. I could do that, so I got five tries my first game."

In 2001, Victoria enrolled in the Auckland University of Technology to study health science-physiotherapy, becoming the first on her mother's side to seek higher education. The course inspired her because of its relationship to sport and because it spared her from being office bound in future, something she was determined to avoid.

Graduating in 2005 at the age of twenty-three, she spent the next thirteen years managing her four physio practices.

During her university years, Victoria got serious about playing rugby when more and more people invited her to join their teams. She brought multiple skills to the game, including agile footwork, full-out sprinting, and the catching and aerial skills sets she learned from netball. An aversion to the contact aspect motivated her to concentrate on scoring tries,[6] at which she would excel. Since she was unaware at the time of women's test rugby, the sport was no more than an enjoyable pastime for Victoria. It was certainly not a career option.

Playing for the Takapuna Rugby Football Club on the North Shore of Auckland exposed Victoria to higher levels of the sport and, importantly, she and her teammates became lifelong friends. During this time, she was recruited to play for the Auckland Marist Rugby Club by Darryl Suasua, who had coached the Black Ferns to victory at the 1998 and 2002 Women's Rugby World Cup. Joining the Black Ferns in 2006 was a turning point in Victoria's rugby career because she had now begun training seriously. Her innate talent blossomed, and she gradually acquired the skills and professionalism required to play international rugby for one of the world's great squads.

"I knew I wanted to play for New Zealand, but I didn't set out to be a Black Fern; it just happened." In fact, Victoria's family weren't supportive of her rugby goals, her mother preferring her to be a Silver Fern, as the national netball team is called. "Rugby was a big no-no, which is probably why I wanted to do it. I have a lot of motivation when I have it hard."

Victoria went on to a stellar international career, playing both fifteens and sevens for the Black Ferns. She was a key member of the squad that won the 2006 Rugby World Cup fifteens in Edmonton, Canada; she played when the Black Ferns placed second at the 2009 Rugby World Cup sevens in Dubai; and she was named vice captain and played starting full-back when New Zealand defeated England 13–10 in the 2010 World Cup fifteens final played at Twickenham

---

[6] A try is scored when the ball is grounded on or behind the goal line in the opposition's in-goal area.

Stoop Stadium. In 2011, she was promoted to team captain for the Black Ferns tour of England and France. All the while she was working full time as a physiotherapist.

Victoria claims that leadership did not come naturally to her. "I was very young in my leadership capacity; it was quite confronting for me, and I felt really nervous. And the promotion came just after the 2010 World Cup, so we lost a lot of experienced players." She was also plagued by an ongoing back injury and took 2012 off. When the injury failed to respond to rehabilitation, she retired from the Black Ferns in 2013.

Victoria, whose maiden name is Blackledge, married her partner Michael Grant, a busy general practitioner, in 2008. For years, he had been supportive of her rugby and physiotherapy careers, both demanding, even though that meant delaying the family both wanted. In 2014, with the birth of their daughter, August Reremoana Grant, Victoria decided to make a major change. "[My husband] loves his work, and I didn't; I was over physio and felt I was getting burned out because I had such a full plate, so I sold my practices, stayed home to look after our daughter, and worked on my coaching, which was starting to pick up."

Building Coaching Credentials, Gaining Experience

Victoria had begun to coach in 2012 while she was a player with the coachless University Club Rugby team based out of Hamilton/Kirikiriroa, having accumulated the necessary knowledge of the game and the skill set to handle the role.

In 2014, following the birth of August, she began coaching in earnest, this time with Rotoiti Rugby Club's premier women's team in the Bay of Plenty/Te Moana a Toi-te-Huatahi region of the North Island, and with the Bay of Plenty Volcanix, the provincial women's team, as assistant to head coach Brad Flemming. Her interview for the latter team had been delayed for several hours as she gave birth but went ahead later in the day. "Before this, my coaching had been community based, and now someone actually wanted me and valued what I brought to the table. I realised that coaching could be something I could do in the future. It was like a lightbulb moment." Over the next several years, Victoria added leadership of the New Zealand U-18 Sevens and the Black Ferns Sevens development team to her credentials.

Victoria Grant is at home on the pitch.

Experiencing the Women Coach Internship Programme

Late in 2017, when Tony Philp, New Zealand Rugby's high performance sevens manager, heard of the WCIP, he told Victoria that her nomination would be supported. She was chosen as one of twenty women coaches from around the Commonwealth, and the programme would bring her to Gold Coast for the 2018 Commonwealth Games, but the experience was more than she bargained for. When a Black Fern contracted the highly contagious mumps, the Black Ferns were initially told they would not be allowed to play, devastating players and coaching staff alike. Eventually, a compromise was reached, and the New Zealanders isolated during the early days of the Games at their training venue on the Sunshine Coast, some 200 kilometres north of Gold Coast. Managing the situation was, Victoria recalls, a huge lesson in coping under pressure.

When the isolation period ended, the Black Ferns moved into accommodations in Gold Coast and continued preparing for the tournament, the last event of the Games. New Zealand outscored Australia 17–12 to win the gold medal, a thrilling outcome that more than compensated for the previous unsettling weeks.

Although being in isolation prevented Victoria from taking full advantage of the WCIP, she nevertheless took away "huge learning" from the sessions she was able to attend. In her exit interview, she described her reality as a woman rugby coach in New Zealand. At that time, there were no women coaches working beyond the provincial level, so navigating a professional pathway was difficult. As well, the sport was heavily male dominated with few female role models.

Recognising the need for change, as of 2016, New Zealand Rugby began arranging workshops for the next generation of women coaches working at the provincial level. "I and a few very good friends all played together and now we are coaching. The provinces have pushed us and are always there for us. It's most difficult at the grassroots level; that's where the stereotypes are ... the clubs are really challenging because they won't listen to a female voice. They all stick together, and we are the minority ... there's the feeling of always having to prove yourself ... I found it difficult as a woman coach in my community ... diehard rugby fans are about fifteens and some don't even recognise sevens, and it's such an awesome game. I hope the narrative continues to evolve to where women coaches are the norm."

Illness Intrudes

Victoria, Michael, and August are country dwellers, living forty minutes from Rotorua on the North Island. Ordinarily not an issue, the distance became a problem in July 2018 when Michael fell deathly ill with a strep infection. Unconscious when he arrived at the hospital, he was put on massive antibiotics. After his discharge two weeks later, the symptoms recurred. A scan revealed that the infection had settled in his heart, requiring open heart surgery with a 30 per cent chance of survival. Then a lack of oxygen to his brain during the surgery resulted in a stroke. "He couldn't move his left side and didn't know me or August; only after a two-year rehabilitation was he able to return to work. Family became number one; it changed some of the things I wanted to do. For me, it was all about helping him to get back to medicine, to be the best he can be."

Victoria's appointment in December 2018 as head coach of the Black Ferns Sevens development team coincided with Michael's rehabilitation, which went better than expected. It was a huge challenge to manage, but she said, "We have a lot of family support who were able to come and stay when I was away."

Timely International Opportunities

Victoria's coaching talents may have been underappreciated at the club level, but they attracted international attention, leading to a four-month stint commencing in March 2019 as the head coach of the Tokyo Phoenix Rugby Club in a countrywide series leading to the Japanese national sevens championships. The timing suited, since Michael was not yet back to work, so he and August were able to accompany Victoria to Japan; being off-season in New Zealand, the offer was supported by the Black Ferns leadership. "It was a good opportunity to be part of a professional environment, to be paid to coach full time, to train every day, and to develop my craft," said Victoria, whose skills were known to the Phoenix team owner, Yohei Shinomiya. It was also, she said, "amazing" for her family to be immersed in the Japanese way of life. August, whose first language is Māori, entered full immersion kindergarten, and by the time the family returned to New Zealand, she understood the Japanese language.

On November 8, 2019, Victoria was one of seven women rugby coaches selected to participate in the Women's Sport Leadership Academy for High Performance Coaching (WSLA HPC), a partnership between the Anita White Foundation, Females Achieving Brilliance, and the Universities of Chichester and Hertfordshire. She was nominated for the programme by Cate Sexton, who was the head of women's rugby at the New Zealand Rugby Union at the time.

Held at the University of Chichester in the United Kingdom and approved by the International Olympic Committee (IOC), the fourteen-month programme reflected the goal of Recommendation 6 of the *IOC Gender Equality Review Project*, which calls for "balanced gender representation for coaches selected to participate at the Games."

The programme, which was delayed by fourteen months because of the COVID-19 pandemic, began with a one-week residential course followed by online tutorials and workshops. Joining Victoria were rugby coaches from Australia, Spain, Wales, South Africa, Samoa, and Hong Kong as well as coaches from cycling, rowing, wrestling, tennis, and triathlon. Goals included "strengthening the female coaching network; identifying sport-specific skills and experience; developing leadership competencies; building confidence; sharing good practice; and developing close links and networks between the participants and international federations."[7]

"WSLA had amazing facilitators from different sports and countries," said Victoria. "It was an awesome journey for me, great to be surrounded by like-minded people who are on a learning journey around leadership and coaching. The other coaches were amazing. I was able to work on my strengths and weaknesses with the support of my leadership mentor, facilitators, and fellow coaches."

Progressing Despite COVID-19

Victoria credits World Rugby with enabling its coaches to manage and even thrive during the pandemic. This is in line with the principle, stated in its *Women Coaching Rugby Toolkit*, that women, who "make up over 25 per cent of the rugby-playing population, should be represented in all areas and at all levels of the game." A list of reasons to increase the number of women coaching rugby included "more coaches with better qualifications and experience ... access to a wider skill set ... untapped

---

[7] International Olympic Committee, *IOC Gender Equality Review Project* (International Olympic Committee, 2018), https://stillmed.olympic.org/media/Document%20Library/OlympicOrg/News/2018/03/IOC-Gender-Equality-Report-March-2018.pdf.

talent ... diversity improves organisational performance ... the quality of decision-making is better ... the presence of women — with different traits, qualities, and life and leadership experiences — may prevent 'bullying' environments ... strong, confident female role models..."

"World Rugby was awesome," said Victoria. "Online Zoom webinars every two weeks for an hour on relevant topics; great speakers, so learning from really good coaches on all aspects of the game; technical information, which we need; and connecting with women rugby coaches from around the world and amazing facilitators who are legends in our game. Having this feeling of connection, even though everyone was far apart, was amazing. The sessions helped me to understand the game better, especially around communications. Being clear and succinct in Zoom is very important, and that challenged me."

Hurricanes head coach Victoria Grant and strength and conditioning trainer Luke Vasu

Within New Zealand, Victoria's development squad programme was put on hold throughout the pandemic with leadership exploring alternative ways to develop players, including inviting selected development players to Black Ferns Sevens development camps. In comparison to many other countries, some play continued, with

Victoria coaching her Rotoiti team at domestic invitational tournaments, but funding cuts related to the pandemic limited pathways for players, coaches, and support staff.

As Victoria pursues her coaching career, she remains a committed mother, learning to balance the necessary time and energy coaching with making sure her family gets the best of her. She sets firm boundaries: Her players know she is available at specified hours; her family knows that her time is theirs when she is home. Her situation is helped by a strong support network that steps in when she travels, providing babysitting and school pickups as needed.

A Future Full of Promise

In November 2021, Victoria, who is the first woman to coach a men's premier rugby side in the Bay of Plenty/Te Moana a Toi-te-Huatahi, won the Farmlands Club Coach of the Year award. "I want to thank the Rotoiti Premier Men for having my back and trusting in me this year. That was massive for me." Looking ahead, she aims to one day coach the Black Ferns, either sevens or fifteens. She also plans to establish a club academy for sevens. "I want to create a pathway for girls to play sevens, from U-8s to an open women's age group. I also see the academy providing a pathway for women rugby coaches to grow and support each other."

In 2022, Victoria added another position to her burgeoning resume after being chosen as an assistant coach with the Hurricanes women's team in the Sky Super Rugby Aupiki,[8] a professional women's rugby union national club competition. Consisting of four teams, the event is a stepping stone between the Farah Palmer Cup (the highest level of domestic women's competition) and the Black Ferns. Said Hurricanes coach Wesley Clarke: "Tors (Victoria) has an astute rugby brain, both as a player and in the coaching space. She has a massive amount of experience at high-level coaching, so she

---

[8] The name Super Rugby Aupiki reflects on the competition being a crucial stepping stone between Farah Palmer Cup and the Black Ferns, with Aupiki translating to mean "the ascent to the uppermost realm."

understands high performance ... she's a great character. She has a great work ethic, and she is a smart cookie both on and off the field."

In September 2023, Victoria took another giant step, succeeding Clarke, who stepped down as head coach of the Hurricanes Poua for the 2023 season. Says the first woman head coach, "I'm excited to be leading the Poua. Stepping up from assistant gives me a great insight into what's needed to progress us forwards. Working with Wes in 2022 was fantastic. Learning off the best. He has left a great platform for us to launch off."

Whatever lies ahead, Victoria's Māori heritage will figure prominently in her actions and decisions. "Māori culture is a huge part of my identity; I strive to live through that identity and every day I learn from August. She is lucky to live where her ancestors are from, and Michael and I are also from where we live. August is surrounded by her extended family every day; she is related to everyone in her class at the local Kura Kaupapa school, the Māori full immersion language school, and I learn a lot from her."

Chapter Three

Dumisani Chauke

South Africa

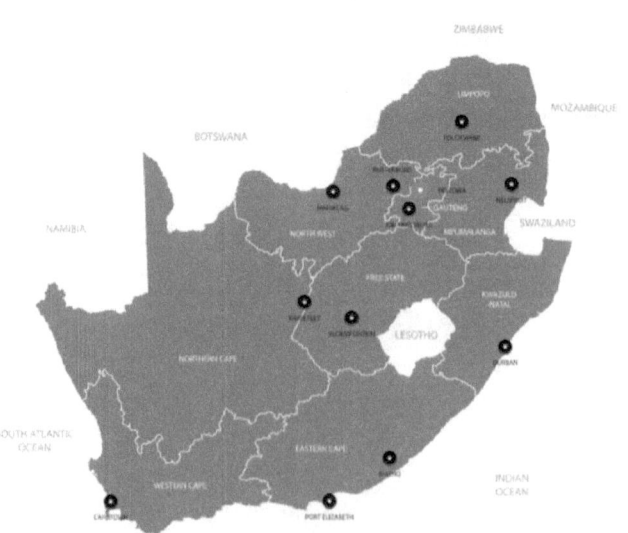

Dumisani Chauke was one of twenty women coaches from around the Commonwealth to be selected for the Women Coach Internship Programme, an innovative initiative of the Commonwealth Games Federation for the 2018 Commonwealth Games in Gold Coast, Australia.

Even prior to the WCIP, Dumi's professional trajectory was accelerating.

On the coaching side, she contributed to the gold medals won at the World University Netball Championship in 2016 and at the African Netball World Youth Cup qualifiers, also in 2016, which secured South Africa a spot at the 2017 Netball World Youth Cup, where the team finished sixth. In 2018, she was head coach of the South African U-20 netball team to the Region 5 Youth Games in Botswana, where the team won gold. In 2019, after a stint as national U-21 assistant coach, she was promoted to the position of assistant coach of the national team (the SPAR Proteas). As head coach of the Gauteng Golden Fireballs, she led her team to a bronze medal finish in the Telkom Netball League in 2020. From 2016 to 2019, she was the head coach of the Tshwane University of Technology (TUT) netball team, which she now supports as its technical director. And she was head coach with the Limpopo Baobabs, which competes in the Brutal Fruit Netball Premier League, now the Telkom Netball League.

On the work front, Dumi has also shown remarkable progress. In 2016, she was recruited by TUT's directorate of sport and recreation as a sport organiser for netball, basketball, and volleyball. Five short years later, in July 2021, she had progressed to being the first female head of department of sport at TUT's Ga-Rankuwa campus. "I'm a part-time coach and a full-time sport administrator, and I have no idea how I manage all of it," says Dumi, who holds a postgraduate diploma in sport management and is working on a master's degree in marketing.

Dumi is a well-known philanthropist committed to improving the lives of girls and young women. Upon her return from the Region 5 Youth Games, she took top honours at the South African Youth Awards in the Sport, Health, and Well-Being category, winning the Presidential Award. In 2019, she was named one of the Top 100 Most Influential Young South Africans in the Social Enterprise and Philanthropy category and finished in twenty-first place. In 2021, she was announced as the latest ambassador of the prestigious Laureus Sport for Good Foundation. "Founded under the patronage of Nelson Mandela, Sport for Good uses sport as a powerful and cost-effective tool to help children and young people overcome violence, discrimination, and disadvantage in their lives."[9]

Dumi is also the doting mother of a son, AJ, born in 2012, and a daughter, Sibu, born in 2019. Fiercely protective of her children, she has mastered managing her multiple obligations, noting that it's hard enough for mothers to be involved in sport, let alone coaching. "Your children are your number one priority, but work is important, so planning and time management become critical if you are to achieve balance. My support system allows me to be a mother, a sister, a sport administrator, a coach, a philanthropist, a netball analyst, and a public figure. It is unfortunate that most women end up stopping their involvement in sport as balancing motherhood and sport commitments can be challenging. But it is doable."

What also helps Dumi is her planning and organisational skills along with the support of her netball family. For example, she brings Sibu to tournaments. "Coaches, players, and other staff take turns looking after her while I'm courtside, coaching." She asked for and received a car seat on the team bus and a hotel room next to the reception desk so Sibu's pram was easily accessible — simple requests that few women coaches think to make but that are vital to combining motherhood and coaching.

Modest Beginnings

Dumi's story began on September 17, 1986, with her birth in the small township of Malamulele in Limpopo Province. Always an active child, she played basketball and football before getting involved in netball around the age of ten. This coincided with her family's move to Polokwane, the capital of Limpopo Province, seeking better employment, better schools, and a better life.

"My parents, Hilda Hlekani Chauke and Thomas Risimati Chauke, worked hard to provide for me and my siblings, Nyiko Chauke and Mikateko Chauke, but as is often the case in small towns,

---

[9] Laureus Sport for Good, "About Sport for Good," Laureus, accessed September 20, 2023, https://www.laureus.com/sport-for-good/about.

there wasn't much in the way of entertainment or activities, so I found my safe place in sport, thanks to my dad, who took me to his football games. I fell in love with the game and eventually started playing it as well as volleyball, basketball, softball and, later, netball."

During a WCIP session in Gold Coast, Dumi was moved to tears by the presentation of Joan Smit, the International Netball Federation's regional development manager for Africa. "It reminded me, first, of the power of sport and, second, it reminded me that so many children in Africa, and in the world, find their safe space in sport. Had it not been for sport, I would not be where I am today, I would not be who I am today, and I would not be telling my story."

As the teenage Dumi watched televised netball games, she began to dream of being one of those players. She was undeterred by serious knee injuries that required reconstructive surgery nor by her doctor who warned she could end up in a wheelchair if she returned to play.

Return she did and, by the age of fifteen, Dumi was chosen for the national U-16 netball team, a tremendous accomplishment for a small-towner. "It was one step closer to being one of the bigger girls…"

Left to right: Griffith intern Sarah Sames, Dumisani Chauke, Isabelle Lindor-André and Grace Mmolai at the WCIP closing reception
Photographer: Murray Rix, Rix Ryan Photography Qld. Supplied by Griffith Uni Gold Coast, Queensland.

However, upon learning the news, the doctor went so far as to urge Dumi's parents to prevent her from playing, to which she replied that playing was her decision. Injured a second time, she insisted that nothing would stop her from playing the sport. "Stubbornness is one of my driving forces. I don't let other people's limitations limit me."

Dumi also excelled at basketball and made both national squads in 2009. Netball won out over football when she was awarded a bursary through Netball South Africa to study sport management at Nelson Mandela Metropolitan University (NMMU) in Summerstrand, Port Elizabeth. She brought to the team a bubbly personality, charisma, leadership qualities, and a never-say-die attitude. "[My teammates] knew that when I was on the court we were bound to win because I had a hard-working ethic, was highly motivated, and was an accurate goal shooter. Get the ball to me and I will put it in."

Transitioning to Coaching

During her playing days, Dumi thought carefully about her future. Being multitalented, she had several options, with coaching a strong possibility. "Coaching came naturally as I enjoyed assisting other players and guiding those younger than me ... Coaching was a way of giving back to the sport."

As a requirement for completion of the practical component of NMMU's sport and recreation module, Dumi started coaching at local primary schools at the age of eighteen, sharing her netball knowledge and earning pocket money. She progressed to coaching at secondary schools and eventually coached the NMMU team, SPAR Madibaz, first as a player-coach with head coach Lana Krige before assuming head coach duties when Krige opted for a break from coaching in 2014 and 2015. That appointment coincided with Dumi's retirement from international netball to concentrate on coaching in 2014. Unsure at first of her readiness for the promotion, Dumi's confidence grew as she gained experience. Around the same time, she became assistant coach of the national U-21 side, working with Dorette Badenhorst.

Initially, Dumi's parents, although supportive of her ambitions, did not think it was possible for her to make a career of sport. Seeing how much their daughter has accomplished, they are now convinced and are rightly proud.

On the Rise Personally and Professionally

Dumi, who makes her home in Midrand, Johannesburg, is the backbone of the Dumisani Chauke Netball Foundation. The pathway dates back to her childhood and the Magangeni Primary School in Malamulele, where she began her long journey with netball and where, on September 15, 2017, she officially registered the foundation as a birthday present to herself.[10] The focus is on making a difference in the lives of young girls in impoverished, rural areas of South Africa. "I go back to where it all started; that's part of remembering where you come from and giving back to your community."

In explaining the foundation's slogan — "Empowering Young Girls" — she mentions three routes to empowerment: netball coaching clinics, life skills sessions, and community-based projects.

As the coaching clinics teach basic netball skills, the girls also acquire valuable teamwork and confidence-building skills that help to ensure promising futures. The clinics also identify girls with the talent to land a spot on a provincial team, which may lead to a netball bursary, higher education and, ultimately, a better life than would be possible in the villages and townships.

The life skills sessions focus on what Dumi and those who volunteer at the foundation have learned through sport: how to manage their time, finances, and personal lives — and how to improve communication skills, goal setting, planning, and motivation. "Yes, I want to teach them netball skills, but they need the life skills to grow into better people."

---

[10] Mbulaheni Ridovhona, "Legendary Netball Player Launches Her Foundation," *Limpopo Mirror*, March 9, 2018, https://limpopomirror.co.za/articles/sport/46319/2018-03-09/legendary-netball-player-launches-her-foundation-.

The foundation's community-based projects include providing participants with everyday necessities, which many cannot afford. The "preloved tekkie drive" collects and cleans old but usable netball sneakers and distributes them along with new socks and sanitary towels. Those who are unemployed or coping with pay cuts receive food parcels. A partnership with SPAR (the nationwide grocery distribution and retail company) enabled the foundation to distribute five hundred feme packs containing sanitary napkins and basic toiletries. "We understand that when girls are clean, they feel good about themselves; in other words, we are addressing the confidence and motivation aspects of our life skills programme."

The impact of the foundation reaches beyond Limpopo to Mpumalanga, North West, and Gauteng provinces. "We are looking to go to rural and destitute areas all over South Africa, and eventually beyond. We do not want to limit ourselves to any specific number and we do not turn anyone away from our clinics and sessions."

In 2020, as a first step to fulfilling her dream of assembling a netball complex near the TUT campus, Dumi purchased a house in Pretoria for her TUT players with accommodation needs but also to address her concerns about their safety. "It's neat, clean, and right next to the campus ... and is key to building camaraderie" — which is important if the team is to achieve its goal of becoming highly competitive.

WCIP: A Turning Point

Dumi has always seized every opportunity to enhance her skills. When the WCIP came along, she needed little encouragement to submit her application. She viewed the WCIP as the ideal opportunity to experience international competition firsthand and to be fully embedded with the SPAR Proteas on the field of play. The Games locale was also appealing. "There was no way I was going to pass on an opportunity to travel to Australia."

Dumi, who applauds the Commonwealth Games Federation for being an influential and critical player in empowering women coaches, came to the Games determined to absorb every possible learning opportunity. She said at the time, "as a young coach, it is very important to have people experienced in netball to mentor and guide me; their wisdom and experiences are invaluable. Meeting other coaches and developing networks and working relationships is of vital importance in enabling coaches to stay in touch and facilitate communication and sharing of information. This is the realisation of a childhood dream. It indicates the endless possibilities that exist within sport…"

Coach Dumisani Chauke in action

The WCIP proved to be a turning point in Dumi's coaching career, giving her the confidence she needed to become a national coach. "I got to sit on the SPAR Proteas bench with the legendary Australian coach Norma Plummer, who led the team from 2015 to 2019 (and has returned to the post in preparation for the upcoming World Cup), and assistant coach Nicole Cusak, another Australian star player turned coach; I got to feel the pressure; I got to feel the fire; I got to feel the excitement, the highs and lows. It made me want this coaching thing even more … there were no limitations."

For Dumi, another strength of the WCIP was the opportunity it provided to share experiences with nineteen like-minded women coaches and their mentors. Most striking were their similarities, despite disparate backgrounds, sports, and environments. The intern coaches quickly and intuitively coalesced into a support group that continues. "We all came with open minds and open hearts, willing to share and willing to learn, and that is why we still talk, still connect, are still laughing —because we became a sisterhood." Taking her place on the bench during the Games was "a huge, huge accomplishment" — which provided the international experience to successfully apply to be the team's assistant coach.

As Dumi progressed, she was still frustrated by the fact that few women hold managerial positions in sport in general and by the failure of her male counterparts to take women coaches seriously. "Women always have to overexplain and prove themselves before being given what they need or the respect they deserve." As well, female codes (sports) are under-resourced when compared to male codes, a situation she attributes to the absence of women at the decision-making table. The pay gap is a further irritant, with male coaches and any coach of male sports earning far more than women coaches.

South African society, splintered by the system of institutionalised racial segregation known as apartheid, which formally ended in 1994, has not been entirely transformed. "Apartheid remains a very thorny issue as its effects are still felt and experienced to this day. I will not say much, but the colour of a person's skin still plays a role in certain spheres, sport included."

Dumi reflected on the personal athletic and coaching milestones that dot her career thus far: making South Africa's U-16 team in 2002 as a fifteen-year-old and representing her country for the first time; the gold medals from the World University Netball Championship and the Region 5 Youth Games in 2016; the WCIP experience; her record as the TUT coach and taking the team from eighteenth overall when she took over in 2016 to top eight in 2019 and a spot at the National Championship, which is televised. "That was a proud moment for me and the girls. Most are from disadvantaged areas and didn't really believe in themselves, so when they found themselves playing netball on TV, they couldn't believe it!" Now Dumi is building even stronger coaching credentials as assistant coach with the SPAR Proteas, ranked fifth in the world in 2022 and a regular contender at World Cups, Commonwealth Games, the biannual Netball South Africa Challenge, and the annual Netball Quad series against Australia, New Zealand, and England.

Like her philanthropy, Dumi's coaching successes have not gone unnoticed. Leading up to the 2019 Netball World Cup in Liverpool, England, where the SPAR Proteas finished a respectable fourth, she was featured in *NetBall Mojo*, a publication which describes itself as an Africa-wide "cool guide to help teenage girls overcome some of the many issues they face as they start to play competitive netball."

In 2019, Dumi was confronted with the COVD-19 pandemic. The impact was "massive," said Dumi, who counts herself fortunate to have a contract which guaranteed her a paycheque even though she was unable to coach. She used the resultant downtime to host her foundation's life skills sessions online, participate in webinars, accept speaking engagements, host events, and release "Coaching from Home" videos for the Netball South Africa YouTube channel, which covers tips on training and developing coaching skills.[11] And in August 2022, she was elected vice chairperson of University Sport South Africa Netball. She expects these varied initiatives, which expanded her profile, broadened her learning experiences, and grew her network, to continue.

While Dumi cannot predict her future, she is clearly a woman to watch — for her coaching journey, her philanthropy, her career as a university administrator, and her avocation as a television analyst for the South Africa–based Super Sport group of television channels. "Anything is possible; the future looks great." Her determination to be at the forefront of decision-making is unshakeable. "When discussions are held around funds, resources, and facility allocations for women's sport, if we are not there to make the decisions, no one will."

---

[11] Dumisani Chauke, "Coaching from Home with Dumisani Chauke | Training Session 20-26," posted May 14, 2020, NetballSA, YouTube, 1:32, https://www.youtube.com/watch?v=6soymS9J-7g.

Chapter Four

Tina Hoeben

Canada

Tina Hoeben did not set out to be a swim coach. In fact, considering her introduction to swimming lessons, the odds were very much against such a career path. "My mother, Bernardina Hoeben, had a sister who drowned, so she was determined that her children would know how to swim. She put us in swimming lessons when we were very young. I have no memories of the first few lessons, but my older sister, Janet Barrett, does and she was traumatised by my crying and refusing to put my head under water; the situation worsened when my mother spanked me in front of everyone...."

Tina recalls this episode when one of her swimmers is struggling. Tina says she's struck by the stark contrast between her inauspicious beginning and her occupation as head coach of the KISU Swim Club in Penticton, British Columbia, a position she has held since 1998. "While there's not a lot of connection between a hard start and where you finish, I have made the sport my life's passion and my career."

On March 18, 1962, Tina was born in Richmond, British Columbia, where her father, Harry, worked at a lumber mill and Bernardina was a stay-at-home mother. Both parents had emigrated from Holland, he in 1953 and she in 1958. Both came from farming families and, in their spare time, managed a hobby farm with a thousand or so egg-laying chickens, a dairy cow, cattle for meat, and various dogs and cats. Tina and Janet had tasks that varied with the seasons but mostly centred around packaging eggs and preparing them for sale.

Not yet a city — that happened in 1990 — Richmond was home to around 75,000 people. Tina thrived in the agricultural environment that surrounded the town, enjoying room to play and seek adventures. When she was ten, the family moved to Summerland, a town on the west side of Okanagan Lake in the province's interior. Her parents were drawn by the prospect of being full-time farmers. There being no pool, the sisters continued their swimming lessons in the lake.

When the community opened its first indoor pool in 1976, despite feeling shy and unsure of herself, fourteen-year-old Tina joined the swim club knowing she had the skill to be competitive and having always wanted to belong to a group. Although a latecomer to the racing side of the sport, Tina was a hard worker who progressed enough to make the varsity team as a distance freestyler when she entered the University of British Columbia (UBC) in 1980. She swam at the national university championships and became team captain.

Intending to pursue a career in medicine, in 1984, Tina completed a bachelor of science degree, majoring in physiology.

Afterwards, to broaden her life experience, she took several years away from her studies to explore the world and read countless novels. Her first trip lasted around six months and took her to New Zealand, Australia, the Cook Islands, and Fiji. "I realised my life had been lived in a fairly narrow environment and I travelled without a particular goal in mind other than to expand my life experiences and what I knew of the world. The first trip, which I did on my own, was fairly safe as the countries were English speaking and not vastly different from what I knew as a Canadian."

For her second trip, Tina travelled with friends, starting out in Turkey, Jordan, and Egypt before moving on to India. It was a very different experience from her earlier travel and influenced her commitment to continue to seek experiences outside of her comfort zone. It also led her to decide to return to university. "My intention was to spend a year or two studying courses that would allow me to read novels and round out my education and then perhaps pursue medicine."

Tina Hoeben shares her knowledge with swimmer Justin Fotherby.

From Science to Art to Coaching

And so, in 1986, Tina enrolled in the University of Victoria's Bachelor of Fine Arts programme, concentrating on art, drawing, and photography. It was a curious choice because art had never been part of her life. Her conversion from the sciences was gradual but became all-encompassing as she added intensive study of art history to her course load, graduating in 1990. By this time, a medical career was no longer an option. "I found I loved many other things as much as the sciences, and the thought of going back to school for many years and having to pay off the debt that would result was unappealing."

Throughout this period, Tina supported herself by coaching summer club swimming. Self-described as "frugal," she always held part-time jobs, including lifeguarding, assisting in labs, and helping to set up exhibitions.

In 1992, Tina added a master's of fine arts degree from York University in North York, Ontario, specialising in sculpture and installations. The life of an artist seemed inevitable, but it would not be in Toronto. "I had my degrees and to some extent had fulfilled the need to travel and experience the world, and I knew if I was going to be unemployed, I wanted to be living near my family; the Okanagan landscape was also very important to me. I had gone to UBC, which is incredibly beautiful, lush, and so close to the ocean. So is Victoria. Living in Toronto, I didn't see water daily and I realised that it is essential for me. Looking over water, swimming in water (not a pool) gives a feeling of awe; it fills the soul. There is something about moving through water that is really good for our minds and our bodies."

After her first year at York, Tina returned to Summerland to spend the summer and focus on making art. That experience proved to have an unexpected consequence in terms of her future. "It sounded wonderful to have all that time for art — and I hated it. I'm an introvert, and I gradually realised how important it is for me to interact with people; I get a tonne of satisfaction from that interaction, but I am not always an initiator. I realised I needed a career that forced interaction if I was to get that satisfaction."

It was after Tina's graduation from York that serious coaching came into play. As an unemployed artist living in Penticton, BC, she turned to lifeguarding and summer club coaching at the city's KISU Swim Club to make a living. Teaching art at Okanagan University College was a career option, but coaching quickly turned into a passion that provided the forced interaction she craved. In 1998, when the head coach position with the winter club was posted, she was the successful applicant. "I don't know if it was a firm decision that this was going to be my career for the next twenty-five years, but I knew it would take a lot to push me in another direction."

Poster for Tina's MFA Thesis Exhibition

Being an introvert has not prevented Tina's coaching career from flourishing. She describes the personality trait this way: "I am shy about speaking up in various situations. I often sit back to see how the situation plays out or I take my time to process things and understand the other person's perspective to make sure my perspective is rock solid before speaking. I may appear slow, but it's that I need time to think things through thoroughly ... I think of myself as being quiet and thoughtful although I love being around vivacious people; I just don't want or need that kind of attention."

While Tina suggests that her relationships with her swimmers may take time to become established, she believes those relationships may be deeper than they would have been if she was an extroverted coach. Of primary importance is ensuring that the swimmers know how much she cares about them. In the early days, she implemented a ten-minute Lecture of the Week. When the old pool was shut down in 2010, limiting time in the water, she was reluctant to discontinue the talks, and cutting into training was not an option. Her solution was thirty-minute talks twice a week before practice, and she continued this when the new pool opened. During Talk Time, technique and upcoming meets are discussed but so is character-building, including what it means to be a good person and a good teammate. Swimmers provide feedback through surveys and by contributing to the conversation. "This approach has helped me to build my team, helped us to become better, and helped create healthy athlete–coach relationships."

Always Learning

Throughout her coaching career, Tina has aggressively pursued professional development in her ongoing quest for self-improvement. "I have a passion for learning; I loved going to school, being in class, having a structure and a goal to better myself." As well as achieving high levels of coaching certification, she seeks relevant conferences and mentors and says that mentors in particular have been part of her steady improvement as a coach and are a significant factor in her education. "To observe what another coach is doing on the deck offers a great learning opportunity. Talking with that coach expands my understanding of why they do what they do." She says she is "very picky" in selecting her mentors.

Because she coaches a relatively small club, Tina avoids university programmes and large clubs when it comes to expanding her knowledge. Instead, she seeks mentors from clubs similar in size to KISU, with proven success records. One such mentor is Michael Brooks, then of the York YMCA swimming programme in York,

Pennsylvania, and now an assistant coach with Neptune Natation in Saint-Jérôme, Québec. After hearing him speak at a conference, Tina arranged to visit Brooks, thanks to funding from Swim BC. "I had to go after opportunities ... I've always felt that mentorships are of great value to moving my coaching forwards. They are so much more than what one can learn in a classroom or from a talk by another coach. The details of how another coach executes their practice, how they communicate and react to their athletes, can't fully be told through words in a classroom setting. It was always important to me to go with an open mind and to take in as much information as possible. When I come home, I try out different things but keep in mind that I don't want to become the other coach but rather steal bits and pieces from what I like and make it my own."

Over and above Tina's proven ability to impart technique and training methods is her commitment to teaching her swimmers to be "good people," which led her to seek out coaches Don and Ron Heidary of Orinda Aquatics in Moraga, California. The twin brothers describe their programmes as "grounded in the enduring values of positive culture and character development," and outline their philosophy in a book entitled *Character First*. Spending time at their club was "significant in changing my coaching," said Tina, who subsequently arranged for Don Heidary to come to Penticton and share his wisdom with her swimmers.

Tina brings to her coaching a deep level of commitment that satisfies on two levels: influencing what happens in the pool as her swimmers improve (posting results) and having an impact on who they are and who they will become (building character). She doesn't define her success as a coach simply by her swimmers turning in fast times, even though that success is essential to her career progression. Just as important are the swimmers who may not be the fastest but who have gone on to do well academically or in their careers or who are committed to giving back to their communities.

Asked to describe her life goals, Tina admitted that while she would be "thrilled" if one of her swimmers earned a spot on an Olympic team (winning a medal would be "incredible") she notes, "I have been fortunate to have some really fast swimmers; most coaches have those, but it's a good coach who holds on to them and makes them great." Certainly, she strives for that kind of success, but it's better, she stresses, to focus on creating a healthy environment for all her swimmers.

Although Tina is now recognised by her peers as a successful coach, closing in on four decades of building expertise and profile, that recognition is recent. The reason, she says, is her club's gradual evolution from producing middle-of-the-road results to building a solid, consistent record of success. Further, her shyness and introversion deterred her from engaging in casual, on-deck conversations with other coaches, and she knew her voice, when she chose to use it, was unheard. Now, "my success has made a difference and I feel I'm seen as more of an equal."

That success has also opened previously closed doors, leading to coaching positions at the 2015 Western Canada Summer Games in Wood Buffalo, Alberta, where she coached British Columbia's men's team; the 2016 Western Canada Games in Swift Current, Saskatchewan; and the 2017 FINA World Junior Swimming Championships in Indianapolis, USA. Tina was groomed for these positions through her participation in the Select Coaches Group, a professional programme created in 2017 by Swimming Canada (SC) to develop High Performance Coaches in Canada. She attributes her selection in part to coaching a small club. "I think I've become the poster child; if all the small clubs could get the results I've been able to get, we'd be setting Canada on fire. One of my goals is to spread that success."

Making the Most of the WCIP

In 2018, SC nominated Tina for participation in the Women Coach Internship Programme, which would run throughout the 2018 Commonwealth Games. Problematically, the WCIP coincided with the Cowichan 2018 BC Summer Games where she was to coach, but Tina managed a delicate juggling act between the two. Supported by her club executive and the parents of her swimmers, she arranged for assistant coaches to handle the trials for the Summer Games and flew to Australia in time to participate in the two-week staging camp that preceded the WCIP. "It was a really amazing experience as I was in a mentorship relationship that enabled me to learn from all seven of the team's coaches. It was really good to see how they conducted themselves on deck, but I also travelled to and from the pool with them and so I got to see the varied dynamics in their interactions with their swimmers. More than anything, this illustrated that there are multiple ways to coach and to be successful."

When the team's IT technician was injured, Tina was assigned the job, which gave her a purpose. "I got to watch all the swimming from the best viewpoint and through conversations started to have a deep understanding of what was happening and how things were handled."

As soon as the Games' swimming sessions ended, Tina was on a plane for Victoria, ready to assume her coaching duties at the Summer Games less than six hours after landing.

In her post-WCIP briefing, Tina said the experience enriched and changed her life, particularly the interactions with women coaches from many different sports and countries, the involvement in a multisport Games, and the "unbreakable bond" that developed between the interns.

Tina has also been part of SC's Female Coaches Group, launched in 2018, and the Advanced Coaches Group, which began operation in 2021 and is made up of coaches SC has worked with in recent years, including many from the Select Coaches Group.

Tina's relationship with the WCIP concept continues through her involvement with Commonwealth Sport Canada's WCIP, inaugurated in August 2020 for three interns and their mentors and expanded in 2021 to include six interns and their mentors. A mentor in both programmes, she said the WCIPs have made her stretch as a coach, first as a mentee and now as a mentor. "The information provided has made me think and rethink how I approach my profession. The interaction with other coaches, both from my sport and from other sports, has also been great to enhance my coaching skills."

Coping Creatively

Like coaches the world over, Tina had to find creative solutions to keeping her swimmers engaged, committed, and fit through the months of COVID-19. As long as the pool was closed, the challenges were many and diverse, contributing to frustration and fatigue. Once back in the pool, the challenges remained, albeit in different forms. She introduced a physical distancing system to minimise contact and found a way to schedule all one hundred competitive swimmers into staggered time slots. Virtual racing against teams from across Canada and Britain provided some compensation for the lack of competition. Perhaps hardest for Tina was the doubling of her administrative workload, which pulled her away from her preference for creative coaching.

Despite the further disruption caused by the Omicron variant in January and February 2022, by midsummer, as mandates were lifted and public gatherings allowed and even encouraged, Tina was able to reflect that those difficult months seemed "such a long time ago." Competitions resumed and spectators were once again filling the stands even as health authorities cautioned that new variants would continue to appear and urged vigilance to limit any spread. At least Tina was back doing what she loves — coaching!

To Change or Not to Change?

Tina lives with her dog, Monty, a delightful companion, especially during upheavals such as the pandemic. Throughout her adult life, she has been active in many sports, including endurance events such as IRONMAN, cycling, and paddling. A lover of the outdoors, she completed the Yukon River Quest, which calls for paddling 700 km in under fifty hours; set the course record for Length of the Lake endurance paddling: 100 km from Vernon to Penticton, BC; completed the Paris-Brest-Paris cycling event, which requires participants to cover 1,200 km in under eighty hours; and has completed the IRONMAN triathlon seven times. She enjoys movies and spending time with her sister, Janet, and her family, who live nearby.

As for her future: "I am really happy with where I'm at. Occasionally, I dream of a job only coaching faster swimmers, but that would mean a move, and moving is one of my hesitations because I live in paradise. It would have to be a very big draw, something really special to take me away from here."

Tina Hoeben

Chapter Five

Laura Kerr Lewis

Northern Ireland

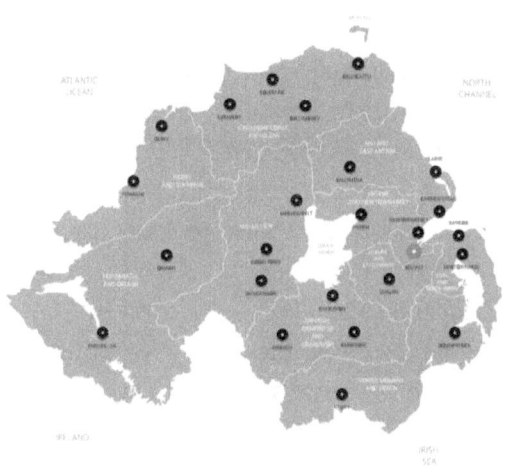

At the time of writing, Laura Kerr was spending what little free time she had in her home, a bare half mile from her parents' farm, where she was raised; she could see the village where they live from the window of her home office. Since her marriage to Stephen Lewis on August 16, 2022, she has lived in a converted barn on the farm as she and her husband build a home they have designed some ten miles away.

As the coach development and talent lead for Athletics Northern Ireland (Athletics NI) from 2014 to 2022, Laura's schedule was hectic.

A cofounder of the Athletics Northern Ireland Youth Academy,[12] which has supported the country's most talented athletes and their coaches since 2014, and the Speed-Power Academy, launched in 2018, Laura explained that the academies "aim to identify and develop talented junior athletes and raise their potential for senior success. The focus is on improving physical qualities, sporting knowledge, psychological skills, and performance behaviours in young athletes whilst educating parents and coaches on what it takes to perform consistently on the international stage as seniors. In doing so, a pipeline of junior athletes will be developed to become successful seniors representing Northern Ireland at the Commonwealth Games and Britain or Ireland at major championships."

Results posted by the junior athletes confirm the success of the academies to date. These include Commonwealth Youth Games medals, European Junior medals, and World Para medals. Encouraging results have been posted at European Athletics Team Championships and European and World Indoor Championships, with twenty-seven Northern Ireland U-20 and U-18 records broken between 2015 and 2022. At the 2022 Commonwealth Games in Birmingham, England, with Laura as team coach, the results were the best for Northern Ireland since 1986 in Edinburgh, Scotland, with two silver medals and four top-eight finishes.[13] Five female graduates of the Youth Academy, all in their early twenties, competed there, with Kate O'Connor winning the heptathlon silver medal. "These results were made all the more satisfactory because I coached Kate between the ages of thirteen and eighteen and there she was, winning a silver medal at the age of twenty-one."

As Laura described her overall role in managing the academies and driving the vision for talent development in Northern Ireland, she pointed to the multiple dimensions involved in preparing teams

---

[12] "Youth Academy & Speed-Power Academy," Athletics Northern Ireland, accessed September 19, 2023, https://athleticsni.org/Athletes/Athlete-Development-Pathway/Event-Group/Youth-Academy-and-Speed-Power-Academy.

[13] "Birmingham Most Successful Games since 1986," *Athletics Northern Ireland*, August 12, 2022, https://athleticsni.org/News/Commonwealth-Games/Birmingham-Most-Successful-Games-since-1986.

for competition. "I reported to a sport governing body, handled coach education, compiled statistics, arranged physiotherapy for forty-five young athletes, managed coaches with multiple programmes, liaised with British Athletics and Athletics Ireland, and I coached three nights a week and on weekends; it was a highly antisocial schedule," she said, laughing.

Laura also handled such leadership roles as team leader of the Britain and Northern Ireland team that topped the medals table at the 2022 European U-18 Championships in Jerusalem. "This event provided an excellent opportunity for athletes and coaches to experience and learn key skills, abilities, and behaviours needed to progress through the pathway and onto the international stage."

A Pastoral Childhood Amidst the Troubles

Born on September 3, 1985, in Lisburn, Northern Ireland, to Gary and Anne Kerr, Laura spent her childhood on the family's beef farm, located in the picturesque village of Ravernet, 10 miles from Belfast and 2 miles from Lisburn. The relative remoteness enabled the Kerrs to live a rural lifestyle of their choosing, and for Laura and her younger brother, Brian, that meant carrying bales of hay, mending fences, and feeding cattle. "The daily physical chores began at three thirty p.m. and had to be done by dinner; we would race to do the tasks. And I became quite strong, especially my shoulders and lifting capacity."

Laura's youth wasn't all hard work, particularly in summer when Anne enrolled the children in multiple camps that exposed them to a wide variety of sports, ranging from badminton and hockey to cricket and athletics. Although active people with a fondness for the outdoors, neither parent could be described as an athlete. The camps, Laura believes, were simply a means to providing the children with an active and enjoyable lifestyle. Equally pleasurable were weekly excursions with Gary, who raced stock cars. "It was inspiring, competitive, and although I was never going to race cars, there was something motivating about the energy and the buzz."

The deadly sectarian violence known as the Troubles was part of Laura's everyday environment growing up in Northern Ireland. From 1968 to 1998, conflict raged between the unionists (loyalists) who desired that Northern Ireland remain part of the United Kingdom, and the Roman Catholic nationalists (republicans) who wanted to join the Republic of Ireland. "The Troubles were part of my upbringing. My family is Protestant, but my parents never instilled any fear in us. In the same way we expected to learn about disasters such as a famine in Ethiopia in international news, so we expected to know about car bombing and bomb scares in the local news. We did hear a few bombs in the distance but never saw an explosion. I always remember my uncle checking under his car for a bomb whenever we went out for ice cream on the weekends. He worked in the army facilities, and so could have been a target. Because I grew up with that, it didn't appear terribly abnormal to me.

"The Troubles weren't about average Catholic and Protestant families; terrorists were at the centre of the Troubles. My parents never encouraged division and have good friends who are Catholic, and many of my best friends at university were Catholic."

Laura's early education began in 1990 at Legacurry Primary School, a small institution in Lisburn with a maximum of nine people per classroom. An excellent student, she was jolted when, at the age of eleven, she didn't do as well as expected on Northern Ireland's transfer test that determines which secondary school pupils will attend. Consequently, she spent the next five years at Laurelhill Community College, which was largely populated by urban students and a sharp contrast to the rural environment she was used to. Adjustment was a challenge. "Initially I was the awkward rural kid who got bullied by my peers. My skirt was too long; I had bigger shoulders and was stronger [than the other girls]; I came from a farming school where we played games in our track suit bottoms every lunch and break time. The Laurelhill girls wore high-heeled shoes and short skirts, and sport was off the table during daytime; that was the biggest shock for me because lunchtime sports had been the best part of primary school."

Fortunately for Laura, girls in Protestant schools were offered hockey and netball during the winter months, with athletics dominating the summer season. Before long, Laura was excelling at sports and academics, which offered some compensation for the bullying. Although she later competed in rowing and weightlifting, Laura shone at athletics, attracted by its individual nature and eager to compete in speed and power events. Determined to win the school's annual Best Athlete award, which usually went to someone who excelled at a run, a jump, and a throw, Laura became an all-rounder and captured the coveted honour. By the age of fifteen, she was national throws and javelin champion and, within a year, she was representing Northern Ireland abroad.

In 2002, Laura transferred to Friends' School Lisburn, one of nine Quaker schools in Britain, not least because sport was offered for A-Level study along with her other preferred subjects: biology, home economics, geography, and physical education. Given the excellence of her grades, medicine or law seemed obvious career routes for Laura to pursue, but being averse to hospitals and blood and unwilling to spend her life behind a desk, neither were a serious option. "I got the Northern Ireland award for my physical education grades, and sport was what I genuinely enjoyed. I was interested enough that sport didn't seem like a job, a chore. It was a pleasure to study all aspects of sport, its history, the science…"

Although Laura was accepted by Loughborough University, regarded as Britain's best for sport, she chose to attend Ulster University, entering in 2004 at the age of nineteen. Not only was it affordable, but internships and scholarships were coming her way, which she partially attributes to coming from a small country. "It's the 'big fish, small pond' effect."

At the same time, Laura was named to Britain's U-23 athletics team as a javelin specialist, earning the prized vest that symbolises that achievement. Progressing further as a javelin specialist remained a goal, but she had begun to wonder if she might be a better coach than an athlete. "I was often too much in my own head, too much thinking about the process, too much writing training diaries, and maybe not enough of a natural flair as a performer ... I was always pursuing a professional career, such as a leadership role in sport science. And so, in my third year, I did a work placement in sport science for the university, earned the Northern Ireland qualification in strength and conditioning, and then added the American qualification and later the British Athletics Sprints and Hurdles group specialist qualification."

Laura Kerr at the 2022 Commonwealth Games in Birmingham, England.

Building the Blocks to Coaching Leadership

Coaching was of particular interest to Laura given the challenges she encountered in finding the right personal coach to support her own development as a competitive track and field athlete. After moving through various coaches between the ages of fourteen and seventeen, she joined forces with retired javelin thrower Alison Moffitt-Robertson, a sports development officer for Ulster University and a Commonwealth Games Northern Ireland administrator, who guided her athletic career until Laura's retirement in 2007 at the age of twenty-two. Alison's coaching tactics, which included systematic annual planning, holistic development, and a focus on technical excellence, suited the feisty Laura, who had a strong sense of what she needed in a coach.

Laura applied her penchant for systems to reversing what she saw as Northern Ireland's chaotic approach to training athletes: using volunteer coaches unfamiliar with sport science. "I was quite driven to make a difference, to make the system a more coherent, organised experience." In 2006, at the age of twenty-one, she added UKSCA Strength and Conditioning Coach accreditation and began working with Northern Ireland's men's volleyball team and archery team as well as with local primary schools. Not yet a licensed driver, Laura relied on her mother for transport. "I thought twenty-five pounds for one hour's work was a lot of money until I realised that my mom had to drive me ten miles north to get the equipment, twenty miles south to get to the schools, and then ten miles north to return the equipment, all for that twenty-five-pound salary. Credit to my parents who knew the work would help me to understand the importance of gaining professional qualifications and experience as well as earning my university degree."

After graduating from Ulster University with a bachelor of science degree in sport and exercise science in 2008, Laura accepted a National Collegiate Athletic Association scholarship to McNeese State University in Lake Charles, Louisiana. It allowed her to return to competition with its athletics team while completing a master's degree in health and human performance, majoring in exercise physiology. She earned the scholarship based on her results as a javelin thrower, which included setting the Northern Ireland record in 2005 at the age of nineteen and earning selection to Team Great Britain. "All through my time at Ulster University, I trained and competed and represented Great Britain and later Ireland at three European Cups. Despite the training, my results didn't get better, and so I retired; I felt McNeese was one last shot to see what I could do."

Laura with marathoners Kevin Seaward and Paul Pollock at the 2018 Commonwealth Games.

Laura's one year of eligibility was extended to two after she was felled by glandular fever. During her time at McNeese, she accepted work in the strength and conditioning departments of women's softball and men's football, enjoying the work but struggling to adapt to the early morning workouts that are an American tradition. "That's not our culture and it was a big shock!"

When the time came to return to Northern Ireland in 2010, Laura was determined to first land a job. A Skype interview with Athletics NI from the McNeese library proved successful, and once home, she commenced a twenty-five-hour a week contract coaching a programme called Active Communities, which catered to people who are isolated and lonely, as well as various other coaching-related jobs. However, her passion had always been performance sport, and when a colleague in that department took maternity leave, she seized the opportunity to switch to her preferred area.

Concerned about the job's transience, Laura was uninterested in a return to Active Communities and was determined to upgrade her credentials. To do so, she crossed the Atlantic once again for a three-month stint at Michael Johnson Performance (MJP)[14] in McKinney, Texas, which describes its programmes as "designed to bring out the potential in every athlete ... with training based on years of research and scientific data."

Although MJP only covered flights, food, and accommodation, Laura was willing to forgo paid work in exchange for exposure to one of the world's best performance environments. Happily living in a motel, she thrived on the structured speed and strength programmes that attracted some of the world's best performance athletes, including players from the National Basketball Association and the National Football League during their off-seasons. Also enrolled were injured youngsters recovering from surgery and children from wealthy families. "The programme let me examine the various demographics of sport, everything from high-paying programmes for kids to top professional integrated sport medicine programmes. I

---

[14] Michael Johnson Performance (website), Michael Johnson Performance, accessed September 20, 2023, https://www.michaeljohnsonperformance.com/.

came back [to Northern Ireland] full of ideas about what I could do. MJP offered me a job, but the position and the money and the working conditions meant I would be struggling."

Laura noted that most of the other MJP employees were engaged in strength, conditioning, and coaching whereas she delved into its business model, its fee structure, the demographics, its marketing model, and how they got buy-in from athletes and parents. "I have always wanted to work my way to the top leadership role of an organisation, and with the MJP experience, I interviewed so much better for my next job at Athletics NI and, once hired, set about implementing my learnings there."

Creating a Thriving Professional Career

In 2014, after her stint at MJP, Laura rejoined Athletics NI as coach development lead and began to develop her career in earnest. Talent identification had always interested her, and she cited the Athletics Northern Ireland Youth Academy as her most significant achievement to date. Working side by side since 2017 with Tom Reynolds (performance lead) was productive. "We shared innovative ideas and drove the sport forwards, creating physical preparation and psychological skills development curricula for the country's best young athletes and their coaches ... at the same time I was driving the idea that coach development and athlete development are one and the same thing. I needed to develop the coaches of the performers, or the performers would not perform."

Participation in the Women Coach Internship Programme accelerated Laura's professional growth. "It was the catapult to get the experience I needed to lead at senior international events and major Games ... it was intensive, on-the-job learning about holding training camps, team dynamics, and integrated service provision." She credited the WCIP with giving her the confidence to assume more leadership roles within Athletics NI, including team management at the World University Games in Napoli, Italy, in 2019. She was subsequently appointed a team leader for Britain at events that, unfortunately, were sidelined by COVID-19.

Laura successfully sought new funding to bolster the Youth Academy programmes. A prime source is Erasmus+, the European Union's programme to support education, training, youth, and sport through grants that provide vocational learning experiences in various European countries as well as a learning curriculum and clear goals. In 2018, she received €120,000 for Youth Academy athletes to attend warm-weather training camps where Laura acted as project manager, which developed her ability to work under pressure and to manage a large team; she later secured an additional €180,000 from Erasmus+, which allowed her to deliver apprentice coach development programmes alongside athlete training camps in Portugal.

When COVID-19 struck, Northern Ireland endured lockdowns beginning in mid-March 2020 and lasting until May, with further lockdowns from September to November 2020, and December 2020 to February 2021; restrictions eased by May 2021. No segment of society was exempt from the pandemic's ravages, and certainly not sport. For Laura, the first hit was a last-minute cancellation of a €60,000 project for more than fifty young people to attend another training camp in Portugal. All travel was banned and a curfew imposed, but local outdoor summer competitions allowed some athletes competing at the senior international level to train at an indoor track and to visit physiotherapists.

For many, the pandemic opened the door to innovation. Laura seized the moment and designed and ran a Zoom series of seven coach development courses featuring international athletics specialists. "The series attracted 1,700 participants from around the world and enabled us to bring the best, cutting-edge speakers who were paid with money from grants, and so we did not have to charge the participating coaches a fee. Everything was incredibly positive, including our international exposure."

Laura's final contribution to Athletics in Northern Ireland was to coach at the 2022 Commonwealth Games, the culmination of eight years of hard work. She agreed that she could be said to be at a career crossroads, although her commitment to optimising performance and coach development remains firm. "As I move to an associate director of athletics role at FirstPoint USA[15] (as of October 2022), my ability to make an impact on young people will continue to grow." Eventually becoming director of Athletics NI has its appeal and could be considered a step up, but for now, Laura is happy where she is. "In terms of what I'm passionate about and what I want to contribute, sitting around a boardroom table is not it at the moment."

---

[15] "Firstpoint USA Appoints Laura Kerr as Associate Director of Athletics," Firstpoint USA, accessed September 19, 2023, https://www.firstpointusa.com/blog/2022/10/laura-kerr-appointed-associate-director-of-athletics/.

Chapter Six
Mildred Gamba
Uganda

It was an early December evening and Mildred Gamba was being interviewed about her life journey so far. Despite an erratic, scratchy telephone line between her home in Kampala, Uganda, and that of the interviewer in Ottawa, Canada, her voice revealed her strong, outgoing, and confident personality.

These traits may be innate, but Mildred's family background has surely contributed to her success as an athlete, coach, teacher, and mother. Finding her place within her family of five older brothers — Gamba Perry, Gamba Tonny, Gamba Ivan, Gamba Nick, and Gamba

Favour — and numerous cousins was a challenge, but one she relished. Her father, Dr. Gamba Osiga, was the district's medical officer and the public sector coordinator of the Project Management Unit of the Global Fund.[16] Her mother, Betty Gamba, was a homemaker, businessperson, and midwife who helped with home deliveries.

For many years, Mildred was the only girl and the youngest child in the family. Her brothers, well known for their sporting prowess, particularly in track and football, were protective of their little sister and spared her the distress of bullying. "Luck was on my side."

Mildred was born on May 9, 1983, in Nebbi, Northern Uganda, a town in the country's West Nile region. Her first sixteen years were spent in the town of Hoima, some 200 kilometres southeast of Nebbi. Hoima, the main municipal, administrative, and commercial centre of Hoima District, has a proud history. Its royal palace, called Ekikaali Karuzika, and the seat of the Omukama (king) of the Bunyoro people, is located there. Nearby are the Mparo royal tombs, the most important being that of Omukama Kabalega, regarded as a hero for fighting British colonial rule in the late 1800s.

In 1962, Uganda gained formal independence from the United Kingdom. In February 1966, Prime Minister Milton Obote suspended the constitution and seized power, abolishing all the traditional kingdoms — including Bunyoro — in 1967. The Omukama of Bunyoro-Kitara Kingdom was reinstated in 1993 in a statute enacted by the Parliament of Uganda. Unlike the pre-1967 Omukama, who was both a figurehead and a political actor in the government of Bunyoro, the Omukama today is a titular head, apart from the functions of the Bunyoro regional government.

For Mildred, the palace and the tombs are familiar symbols of a proud past. "When the Bunyoro kingdom was reintroduced, schools throughout the district, including mine, would take turns cleaning the palace. I was around for the first coronation in 1993, although as

---

[16] The Global Fund to Fight AIDS, Tuberculosis and Malaria, "About the Global Fund," The Global Fund, accessed September 19, 2023, https://www.theglobalfund.org/en/about-the-global-fund/.

a ten-year-old, I can't remember much. I do remember that we were extremely excited about the Empango,[17] the celebration of the coronation anniversary."

Mildred's childhood was carefree. "Growing up in the countryside on the family farm was amazing. Everything was natural with few restrictions. We could freely visit friends, gather fruits, and play. We had a huge compound, and I planted beans, maize, groundnuts, and bananas to help feed the family."

Meals were fresh, healthy, natural, and varied. Most of the foodstuffs came from the farm and included cassava flour bread; rice; sweet potatoes; indigenous greens such as boo, a green vegetable with a strong aroma; dodo, a form of spinach; nakati, a salty and bitter green; okra; pumpkin; cassava leaves; and varieties of fish, meat, beans, and peas.

Mildred attended Hoima Public Primary School, 1 kilometre from the Gamba family home, so within walking distance. She and her brothers usually returned home for lunch but, occasionally, she would join her friends for lunch at the local market to feast on boiled yams, fried cassava, or Ugandan-style pancakes, called kabalagala, made from cassava flour and ripe bananas. Recess, lunch breaks, and after school meant playing games such as skipping, Kwepena (a form of dodgeball dating back over centuries), and dool (a traditional Ugandan game that is similar to marbles). Visiting friends was a favourite weekend pastime. "The grandmother of one friend had a sugar cane plantation, and all of us would go there and enjoy sampling the cane."

---

[17] "Tradition of Bunyoro's Empango," Culture and Traditions, Kabalega Foundation, accessed September 19, 2023, https://kabalegafoundation.org/about-bunyoro-kitara/culture-and-traditions/tradition-of-bunyoros-empango.html.

Mildred Gamba speaking at the WCIP closing reception.
Photographer: Murray Rix, Rix Ryan Photography Qld. Supplied by Griffith Uni Gold Coast, Queensland.

A Lifetime of Sport

Play merged into sport as Mildred was growing up, but it was an activity she enjoyed, not a pursuit that could lead to a career. "I used to run in primary school, but never took it seriously. I just did it for sport's sake since sport was compulsory." Moving to Kampala after middle school, she attended St. Catherine Secondary School for O-Levels, and Makerere High School Migadde, also in Kampala, for her A-Levels, which she completed in 2001. Since the only game available was basketball, she took a break from sport until enrolling at Makerere University, where she participated in interhall competitions as a sprinter, never losing a race. "My early training involved being part of the school team and working with the physical education teachers; I was involved in all sports, including softball, netball, basketball, and swimming, which is how my talent developed."

Mildred had always been fascinated by finance and wanted to work in a bank or other financial institution. She graduated in 2005 with a bachelor's degree in economics. Unable to immediately find a job in the field, she decided to start training as a sprinter.

Throughout her life, Mildred's father was a constant source of support. "He stood with me through it all, especially after university." Support also came from her friends and her coach, Noah Ssengendo, the national sprint coach who is a physical education teacher and head of swimming at Rainbow International School Uganda, located in Kampala. "He always encouraged my sprinting career; he wasn't paid, yet he was always there for me despite his family and work responsibilities."

In 2006, Mildred landed a track scholarship at Western Kentucky University in Bowling Green, Kentucky, and spent an uneventful year there. "Living in America was not much different from Uganda, except that I missed the organic food and communal living."

After the death of her mother in December 2006, Mildred decided to return to Kampala. Enroute home, she stopped over in Britain and signed with the London-based Shaftesbury Barnet Athletics Harriers for one year. While there, she investigated the possibility of staying to train for the 2012 London Olympic Games. Because Britain's visa requirements did not include sport, her request for an extension was denied and she continued on to Uganda.

Upon Mildred's return in 2008, Ssengendo connected her to Rainbow International School, whose physical education teacher was resigning, creating a vacancy for which Mildred was the successful applicant. Thus was her teaching career launched.

Throughout this time, Mildred continued to develop into one of Uganda's top sprinters. Her goal was to be the best sprinter possible and to represent her country at international competitions. "What I like about sprinting is that it gets done very fast. Also, my muscular build suits sprinting."

Before long, the international exposure Mildred craved began to materialise. At the 2006 All-Africa University Games in Pretoria, South Africa, she posted respectable fourth-place finishes in both 100-metre and 200-metre races along with an unlikely gold medal in shotput. "Uganda had no one in shotput so I said I would do it.

Throwers are big and, as a sprinter, I am quite small. People were saying, 'Look at this tiny girl. What is she going to do?' With my first throw I was in top position, shocking everyone. And the gold medal was mine!"

In 2009, Mildred competed at the World University Games in Belgrade, Serbia, in both the 100 metres and 200 metres, the first Ugandan woman to qualify for the semifinals in both events. Her time of 11.2 seconds in the 100 metres easily bested the qualifying mark of 11.7 seconds for the African Senior Athletics Championships. In 2010, she travelled to New Delhi, India, to compete at the Commonwealth Games. "Travelling, we spent twenty-four hours in Dubai International Airport, and I had the hundred-metre heats in two days. There was no time for acclimatisation, and I didn't proceed from the heats."

In 2011, Mildred won gold in the 100 metres and silver in the 200 metres at the national championships held in Kampala's Namboole Stadium. At the time, she publicly deplored the lack of public support for the event. Asked how frustrating it is to win a race and celebrate alone, she replied: "Very frustrating; it is not motivating at all."

One year later, Mildred qualified for the eighteenth African Championships in Porto-Novo, Benin. She was one of four Ugandans to compete at the 2013 Islamic Solidarity Games in Palembang, the second largest city on the Indonesian island of Sumatra.

Mildred's racing career was interrupted briefly when she gave birth to her son, Ibrahim, in November 2014 at the age of thirty-one. She repeated as national 100-metres champion in 2016 and was again named to Uganda's team to the 2016 African Senior Athletics Championships in Durban, South Africa.

Adding Coaching to the Career Mix

Before Mildred joined the Rainbow School in 2008, she was temporarily unemployed, so Ssengendo suggested she coach one of his junior athletes. Later that year, when she was hired as Rainbow's physical education teacher, her responsibilities included coaching all the sports the school offered. As if being a full-time teacher, athlete, and mother wasn't enough, in 2014, Mildred decided to found the Tartan Burners Athletics Club (TBAC) as a means to empower girls through sport. The club relies on contributions from its members with projects being funded by the US Mission in Kampala.

In 2018, for example, the US Mission funded a two-day TBAC empowerment camp for female athletes designed to build their self-esteem. Also funded was a one-year trial project for camps to be held throughout Uganda, with Mildred as project coordinator. "Skill alone is not enough; girls can accomplish whatever they want through perseverance and commitment ... when you are empowered, you can stay longer in school and become an independent woman. Every man desires to have such a wife, and the women will never be vulnerable because they are independent."

TBAC holds empowerment camps throughout Uganda and offers motivational talks, team-building and sports activities, mentorship, sports nutrition, HIV/AIDS awareness, and safety classes aimed at countering the country's widespread sexual abuse and harassment problems.

No subject is taboo. For example, during an empowerment camp, girls raised the challenges of missing classes and sports because of their menstrual cycles and the prohibitive cost of sanitary pads. Mildred decided to offer camp participants reusable sanitary pads "as a means to empower them to continue with life normally and to make them comfortable ... to most girls, periods make them vulnerable to many issues ... the situation is exacerbated by a lack of education on hygienic menstrual practices and reproductive health..."

The camps also encourage achievement of academic goals. "Uganda lacks specialised coaches, so TBAC offers high-quality training that prepares sprinters and long jumpers for better career and scholarship opportunities." Urged by Ssengendo to learn to self-coach, Mildred uses herself to test her training programmes. "My goal is to produce athletes who have excellent technique, are mentally strong, know their strengths and weaknesses, and never give up no matter how tough the situation."

A WCIP Beneficiary

Late in 2017, Mildred learned that the Women Coach Internship Programme would be a component of the 2018 Commonwealth Games. When told that her nomination by the Uganda Olympic Committee was accepted, her reaction was joyous. "I'm going to Australia! I'm going to Australia!"

The WCIP provided Mildred with unique opportunities to enhance her coaching skills. Sprinters were among the first Ugandan athletes to arrive in Gold Coast. Assigned to travel with them, she was given coach, team leader, and team manager responsibilities until the rest of the team arrived a week or so later. "I learned skills I would otherwise never have had the opportunity to do. Making sure the athletes trained, registering the entries, handing out the uniforms, handling protocol — all that was needed, I did it. I think the quality of the work I did gave the leadership the confidence for me to take a team of five women to the World Relay Championships in Yokohama, Japan, in May 2019."

Three months later, at the All-Africa Games in Rabat, Morocco, she worked with the women's 4x400 metres team that broke the national record when they won the bronze medal. With these results, more and more sprinters were being referred to her for training.

"It meant the world to me to be part of the WCIP. I shared knowledge with trained and experienced coaches and got training to develop my young coaching career. The mentoring enabled me to talk to and interact with the best coaches in the world. And networking! Now I stay in touch with people who can help to further my career."

Opportunities and recognition came Mildred's way after the WCIP concluded. She was trained to deliver the World Athletics' Level 1 coaching course at TBAC and continues to coach U-16 athletes from various clubs in their quest to become future track stars. In 2018, the Uganda Athletics Federation appointed Mildred to its Athletes Commission, she was named one of the most influential women administrators in Uganda, and she won second prize in the sports category at the Women4Women Awards. This led to her mentorship by UN Women Uganda — which, according to its website, is part of "the United Nations entity dedicated to gender equality and the empowerment of women."

In October 2019, the US Mission nominated Mildred for its global mentorship initiative and awarded TBAC three grants to run the following: a baseball camp celebrating the legacy of Jackie Robinson and nonviolence; a tennis camp celebrating Arthur Ashe and HIV/AIDS awareness and empowering girls through sports; and a sprinters' camp celebrating the legacy of Wilma Rudolph and overcoming adversity in life.

Mildred decided to continue her own training, inspired by Olympic and world champion Shelly-Ann Fraser-Pryce's presentation to the WCIP in which she talked about returning to competition after giving birth with a more relaxed approach to her training and a newfound motivation to compete.

Inspired by Dumisani Chauke of South Africa (see Chapter Three), Mildred began developing the Gamba Athletics Foundation: "My dream, my passion [is] ... to support the talented girls who belong to the TBAC by connecting them to better schools and scholarship opportunities in Uganda and the United States, better coaching, providing necessities, and mentoring. I have a goal in life to help female athletes achieve their full potential."

Coping with COVID-19

Mildred's intention was to retire from competition to concentrate on coaching and the foundation, but the pandemic upended her plan to launch her foundation in 2020. With some free time on her hands, she decided to work on her weaknesses as a sprinter with a view to eventually returning to competition once the pandemic ended.

As a physical education teacher, Mildred found online coaching a challenge as she tried to balance work and home responsibilities. Concentrating on three athletes, she designed their programmes to encourage independence and focused on general fitness that could be practised at home. Through it all, she remained positive, recognising that the pandemic affected virtually everyone. Best of all, she was able to spend quality time with Ibrahim, assuming the role of his teacher during Uganda's lockdowns: thirty-two days beginning on March 18, 2020, and a forty-two-day partial lockdown from June 7, 2021. "Being his teacher gave me a better insight into his learning abilities; he was six and still learning to read and spell. And it helped our relationship, which is very close. He keeps me entertained and is my training partner. I put him a few metres ahead and chase him. He is very fast and a natural sprinter."

Mildred Gamba coaches many sports at many levels.

A Giving Future

Mildred is a World Anti-Doping Agency educator and a World Athletics lead trainer focusing on youth. She dreams of travelling the world as an international teacher for four or five years, after which she plans to focus on developing the foundation into a formidable vehicle for change. The foundation is registered; the membership and framework are established. She expects it to be fully functional by 2026. "When I look back twenty years from now, I want to be recognised as a person who contributed to the development of athletics and the empowerment of women in Uganda."

That contribution may be hampered by the challenges she encounters as a woman coach, but which she is determined to surmount. According to Mildred, traditionally, a woman coach is given an assignment with the national team only if at least one of the athletes is female. Even then, the position is usually that of an assistant, making it difficult to build a successful coaching resume. Equally frustrating is being "undermined and expected to know less" because she is a woman, a reaction she encounters all too frequently.

Mildred, who has completed a master's of education from the University of the People (uopeople.edu), continues to be positive and upbeat. She hopes that the promotion of peace and education through sports will help girls to realise their potential and encourage them to achieve their academic goals. "Taking part in sports gives girls an opportunity to preserve human dignity and become positive role models in their communities. I am proud to continue TBAC empowerment programmes for as many girls as possible and create not just top sportswomen, but better and safer communities for all women."

Chapter Seven

Soraya Julaya Santos
Mozambique

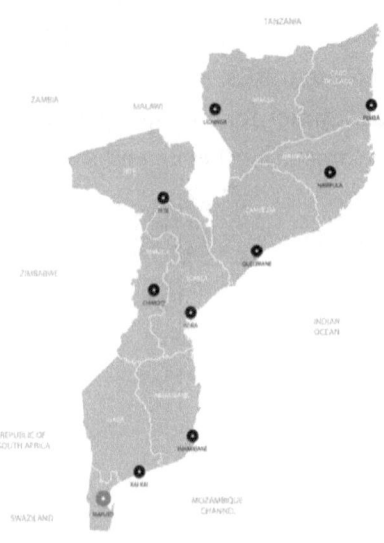

Soraya Santos was one of twenty women from across the Commonwealth selected to participate in the Commonwealth Games Federation's Women Coach Internship Programme during the 2018 Commonwealth Games in Gold Coast, Australia. Her selection proved to be a turning point in a life marked by challenge, joy, and tragedy that included teen marriage, having four sons, early widowhood, single parenthood, and surviving in a male-dominated society. She has been sustained by strong family support and a determination to make a career as a swim coach.

Soraya's country, the Republic of Mozambique in Southeast Africa, was a colony of Portugal for over four centuries, beginning when the explorer, Vasco da Gama, arrived on its shores in 1498; settlement began in 1505. In 1975, Mozambique gained independence and became a one-party socialist state named the People's Republic of Mozambique. The period between 1977 and 1992 was marked by the Mozambican Civil War, fought between the ruling Marxist Mozambique Liberation Front, the anticommunist insurgent forces of the Mozambican National Resistance, and several smaller factions. A new constitution, adopted in November 1990, created a multiparty state with periodic elections and guaranteed democratic rights. The war formally ended in October 1992 with the signing of the Rome General Peace Accords. Periodic violence continues to erupt in the northern province of Cabo Delgado where an armed group sometimes abducts people and destroys homes. More than 735,000 have fled since the insurgency began in 2017.[18]

While Soraya deplores the violence, she is relieved that it is confined to Cabo Delgado, which is over 1,500 kilometres from her home in Maputo, the country's capital.

Although the 1990 constitution grants equal rights to women and men, in practice, gender equality is debatable. According to the World Atlas website,[19] "Gender-based roles are clearly defined in Mozambican society. While men are regarded as the breadwinners, women are expected to manage household chores and engage in childcare. Although women in the rural areas participate in agricultural activities, they are still regarded as subordinate to men and get lower wages. Women in urban areas are mostly confined to the home. Although times are changing, Mozambican women still have a long way to go before they are regarded as equal to men in society."

---

[18] United Nations, "Thousands Continue to Flee Violence in Cabo Delgado," UN News, March 22, 2022, https://news.un.org/en/story/2022/03/1114412.
[19] Oishimaya Sen Nag, "The Culture of Moazambique," WorldAtlas, January 23, 2019, https://www.worldatlas.com/articles/the-culture-of-mozambique.html.

As reported by the Borgen Project in 2018, "Mozambique ranked 139th out of 159 countries on the Gender Inequality Index of the United Nation's Development Programme. While 94 per cent of girls enrol in primary school, only 11 per cent continue to study in secondary schools even though, as of 2003, these schools offer free tuition. Only 28 per cent of females know how to read and write compared to 60 per cent of males. Teen pregnancies are a major reason for girls leaving school early, with 30 to 40 per cent becoming pregnant before the age of eighteen. Child marriages are another roadblock to education with almost half of girls married before the age of eighteen and 15 per cent before the age of fifteen, forcing them to drop out of school."

Soraya Julaya Santos

Overcoming Certain Odds

Determined and committed, Soraya managed to buck many of her country's inequities. One of only three women swim coaches in Maputo (2017 population: just over 1 million), hers has been a circuitous route to her present occupation. She was born on March 10, 1979, in Nampula (the country's third largest city, located roughly 200 kilometres inland from the Indian Ocean), to a Christian mother, Ana Maria Xavier, and a Muslim father, Abdul Rachido Julaya. Soraya's mother was the first of Abdul's three wives and gave birth to four children — Soraya and three sons, Julaya, Micail, and Haider. The other wives had three sons and three daughters between them. When her parents separated, Soraya and her brothers went to live with Ana Maria's Christian family, although it was agreed that the children would be raised in the Muslim faith. (Soraya is a practising Muslim who wears a head scarf when she prays on Fridays and during Ramadan.) However, living in a Christian environment enabled her to play sports while growing up. Her uncles, avid sportsmen who enjoyed football, hockey, and swimming, were inspirational role models as was her mother, who had been a track and field athlete when she was a youngster.

Soraya acknowledges that, as Mozambican girls grow older, they carry an increasing domestic workload and responsibilities. "After the school day, girls have to learn how to do housework and cook as well as keeping up with their schoolwork; boys, on the other hand, have fewer tasks and therefore have more free time. As well, there are more sport facilities and opportunities for boys who are always given priority while a girl only gets a space if one is left over."

Soraya's youth was spent on her grandparents' farm about forty minutes from Nampula City. On a typical day, she woke at 5:30 a.m., showered, and prepared to go to her school, which had big windows, ten classrooms, and a treed and spacious playground. She began her schooling at the age of five; among her favourite subjects were the ABCs, the Portuguese language, and mathematics. Returning home for lunch, she did her schoolwork, played, showered again, helped to prepare dinner, and then went to bed.

While sport was not part of her school's curriculum, exercises were, and so was dance, running, and games. Games were also played after school, including ball games; Police and Thief, a puzzle game whereby the player captures a thief on the loose; and the Goat Game, which is a game of tag between a blindfolded goat and a circle of players. Board games, cards, and Nintendo Game Boy were other diversions once homework was finished. "Even though most girls do, I didn't have chores after school, only studying and homework because we had a nanny and a housekeeper. It was a normal childhood with not so many responsibilities. Occasionally girls and boys played together, but mostly we played separately."

In Mozambique, primary education in public schools is free and compulsory and begins at the age of six. Lower primary consists of Grades 1 to 5, and upper primary comprises Grade 6 and 7. From there, Soraya attended Liceu Alvorada, a private school in Maputo, then Chaimite Secondary School in Beira, a city in central Mozambique. The curriculum included mathematics, history, fiscal policy, biology, Portuguese, English, and chemistry.

Swimming entered Soraya's life at a young age, influenced by her oldest brothers, Haider and Micail, and her uncle, Anselmo Xavier, who were swimmers and would take her to the local pool. Inevitably, she began swimming lessons, not intending to become competitive but as a safety measure. "I did not think that one day I would be a swim coach — I planned to become a schoolteacher — but I wanted to play with the other kids, and I enjoyed being at the pool with them."

During Soraya's teenage years, a frequent visitor to her home was a swimmer and national swim coach named Frederico dos Santos, who was a friend of her uncle Anselmo. Soraya and Frederico became life partners and, at the age of eighteen when she found herself pregnant, they married and moved to Lisbon where Frederico was enrolled in a five-year Level 4 coaching certification course given by the Portuguese Swimming Federation and was also employed as a swim coach. Ricardo was born thereafter, and the family would grow to include Rui, Abdul, and Carlos.

Putting aside her plans to become a teacher, Soraya decided to learn how to teach youngsters to swim and, eventually, she became a volunteer coach working with Frederico. For the first five years of their marriage, they lived in Lisbon. Because she had a nanny, she was able to complete a programme offered by the swimming federation to become an accredited swimming teacher, which meant she would be paid. "I liked teaching how-to-swim classes because a youngster comes to you not knowing how to swim, and some may fear the water, and so you work with them and teach them to like swimming."

Adjusting to motherhood far from home proved to be a challenge for Soraya. "I was young, and I was alone with one child and then another without my mom and my family. That was the hardest part. But when my husband finished his studies, he wanted to return to Mozambique to share everything he had learned about swimming in Portugal. Everything he did at the time was swimming, swimming, swimming, and that is why I did swimming too."

To accelerate her progress from teaching swimming to coaching, and encouraged by Frederico, Soraya was determined to acquire the necessary education. In 2013, she completed the Level 1 coaching course given by the Portuguese Swimming Federation.

She later took the Level 1 coaching course offered by the Fédération International de Natation (FINA), followed by the American Swimming Coaches Association Level 1 and Level 2. Next came admission to the Pedagogical University of Maputo's Faculty of Physical Education and Sport where she studied sports management from 2013 to 2016. In 2014 came her appointment as Frederico's assistant coach at the Tubarões de Maputo Sports Club.

A typical day began with Soraya rising at 4:00 a.m. to organise her household. She woke the children at 5:00 a.m. and readied them to be at her mother's by 5:30 a.m. (Soraya was able to leave the children with her mother while she coached.) She taught a class at the pool until 6:45 a.m. and then went to morning practice until 10:30 a.m., after which she returned home to prepare meals. At noon she picked up the boys from school and they returned home to eat lunch, rest, do schoolwork, and study. She was back at the pool by 2:30 p.m. for another training session lasting until 5:30 p.m.; then it was home to make dinner, go for an evening walk, watch television, and go to bed at 9:30 p.m.

Tragedy Strikes

On February 20, 2016, life changed forever for Soraya and her young family. Tragically, Frederico died after a wall at the entrance of the Zimpeto Olympic Pool collapsed on his car at the end of the Maputo Summer Championships. Soraya and her son Rui were injured in the accident. "When the accident happened, we were taken to the hospital where my brother, Micail Julaya. who is a doctor, received me. He told me that now I had to be strong for my children. An hour later, he told me that Fred was gone but my children were alive and would need me even more now that they were without a father. I did everything I could so my children would not suffer too much. We all went back to our normal activities, and we had psychological help, which was very useful. I continued to do my work, and I had to do it the best way possible because that was my only income."

Making the Most of an Unexpected Opportunity

Soraya's participation in the WCIP at the Gold Coast Commonwealth Games came about when her local swimming association submitted her nomination to the Mozambican Swimming Federation (MSF), whose members approved it and forwarded it to the Commonwealth Games Federation's selection committee.

The WCIP marked a turning point in Soraya's coaching career. "It was especially important to me because I had never had anything big like that. Here in Mozambique, maybe because I am a woman, I had never been chosen to be head coach. [Officials] never saw me as being able to coach a men's team; they thought I should coach with a male coach and be his assistant, even if the head coach was not as good as me."

Soraya's first few days in Gold Coast were marked by a lack of support from the Mozambican coach, who seemed unclear about why she was there. Forced to carve out a role for herself, she devised an acceptable plan guided by WCIP leader Sheilagh Croxon and Mozambique's chef de mission, Afra Ndeve, who facilitated communication with the coach, making him aware of the WCIP and Soraya's role within it.

"The WCIP was a chance for women coaches to show our worth, to show people that we are capable, that we are strong. I learned that I must say what I want and not to always say yes, especially when I know things are wrong. I had to show that I can do the work, and that wasn't easy, but I did it!

"Now the federation knows my work and knows that I am a good coach. When we have our championships, the MSF comes to observe what we are doing and so they recognise that I have talent as a coach ... that I am determined and firm, that I like challenges and don't give up easily."

Soraya did so well in Gold Coast that she was one of three nominees for Mozambique Coach of the Year in 2019. She was chosen as the main coach to represent her country on the African Swimming Confederation (CANA), and she was head coach of Mozambique's team at the 2019 CANA African Championships in Windhoek, Namibia.

"Before Gold Coast, I never had opportunities [with the MSF], but afterwards, when the MSF makes teams to go to championships, they sometimes include my name as a head coach or for some other position. Now they remember my name and that is good."

Daily, working closely with Rui Xavier, the technical director of the Tubarões club, Soraya and the club's other five coaches — she is the only woman — share responsibilities, and each has an equal voice. She and one other coach share the workload for a squad of fifty swimmers aged eight to fifteen. Soraya trains her group of twenty of the youngest swimmers and has the authority to manage their programmes as she sees fit. "My goal is to teach them to be focused, disciplined, humble, able to fulfil the goals I set for them, and to be good companions for each other."

Soraya is determined to always do her job with "great dedication, to gain more and more autonomy in coaching [her] squad, to have more and more swimmers improve their times and break records, and to acquire more coaching knowledge." She is also interested in branching out to coach other aquatic sports, such as water polo.

Soraya Julaya Santos at the Tubarões Club in Maputo.

COVID-19 Hits Hard

According to UNICEF, "the COVID-19 crisis brought new challenges to women and girls around the world and many countries recorded a surge in domestic violence, resulting from confinement and increased tensions in the household. In Mozambique, economic pressure, loss of livelihoods and disruption in access to health, social and protection services placed an added burden on women and girls."

In its efforts to halt the rapid spread of the disease, the Mozambican government, led by President Filipe Nyusi, enacted a number of restrictive measures, including closing establishments selling alcoholic drinks, cinemas, theatres, museums, galleries, discotheques, casinos, gymnasiums, and swimming pools; sharply reducing opening hours for restaurants and shops; closing beaches to swimming and the practice of any sport, although small groups were allowed to walk along them; and restricting attendance at private events (along with mandatory closing at 8:00 p.m.). National sports championships were allowed, but were closed to the public.

Many parts of the country were already in dire straits because of deadly weather events. Cyclone Idai made landfall on March 14, 2019. A Category 4 storm, its heavy rains and intense winds led to flash floods, hundreds of deaths, and massive destruction of property and crops. Six weeks later, equally destructive Cyclone Kenneth hit northern Mozambique. Then, on December 20, 2020, came Tropical Storm Chalane; and in 2022, five consecutive tropical cyclones — Ana, Batsirai, Dumako, Emnati, and Gombe — struck Mozambique and left more death and destruction in their wake.

Although Soraya and her family were not directly affected by the storms, she is concerned about the increasing frequency of such events. "These disasters were far from Maputo, but it is still very sad what happened there. Every year the people suffer as we have had very bad weather. One moment the weather is rainy and then the sun comes out; it is very strange." Many climate experts attribute the increase in storms to climate change, pointing out that, less than five years ago, there were only one or two such storms in the region each year; fifteen years ago, the average was just one each year.[20]

Before the pandemic reached Mozambique, Soraya's coaching was going well, but with the restrictions, life as she knew it came to a halt. The first case was confirmed in March 2020, leading to the first wave; the second wave in April 2021 was followed in quick succession by the third wave in June 2021. "It was overwhelming, the situation got worse with cases increasing every day. Earlier, children and young people weren't affected, but that changed. This time most sports were prohibited, but not swimming if we followed all the rules, and the swimmers were vaccinated.

---

[20] "Southern Africa Storms Fuelled by Climate Change - Study," BBC News, April 11, 2022, https://www.bbc.com/news/world-africa-61067254.

"Our lifestyle had to change, our wages were reduced by half, we had to live with less, and food and other [essential] items got very expensive. Our club fought to show people that swimming is good, that we were being careful and following FINA's COVID rules, but it wasn't easy to convince [the authorities]."

Throughout, Soraya stayed connected to her swimmers using WhatsApp. She urged them to exercise so they wouldn't gain weight. "I asked them to not just stay home, eat, watch movies, and play video games, which they like to do. It didn't help much, but I tried."

Moving Forward

During COVID-19, Soraya worried about what the future held for her and her sons. A project to build her own swimming pool was put on hold indefinitely, and so she took orders for cakes and snacks, which she made herself, and that helped to pay the bills. "I must work to support my sons, and so we had to learn to live with COVID-19. Once we had the vaccine, we were all vaccinated and returning to normal life." Now, Soraya is back coaching full time and life is again stable.

Another concern focused on the departures of young Mozambicans to greener pastures. "Many go wherever they can — Portugal, Brazil, England, America. We are not a poor country, but we have people who are very rich and those who are very poor, and things are not equal for everyone. Of course, I hope my sons will stay in Mozambique, but if they want to go, what can I do? It's their life."

Chapter Eight

Amanda Booth
England

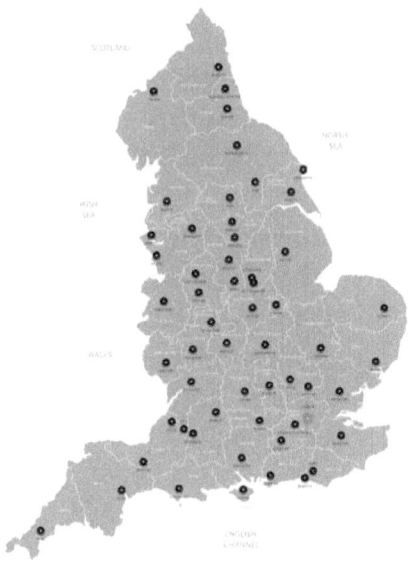

Amanda Booth was born in England on July 10, 1964, and moved back and forth between England and Nigeria multiple times before returning to Britain as an adult to pursue dual careers in coaching and physiotherapy.

Amanda and her younger sister Heather moved with their parents, Colin and Rosemary, to Ewekoro, Nigeria, in 1965, when Colin, an engineer, accepted employment with Blue Circle Industries, a British cement manufacturer. The company was at one time the world's largest cement concern, with holdings in numerous countries, until it was acquired by French company Lafarge in 2001. Just under 70 kilometres inland from Lagos, Ewekoro remains a hub of cement production.

The family went to Yorkshire in 1968 for the birth of Amanda's brother, Michael, returning shortly thereafter to Nigeria. Three years later, suffering from morning sickness and unable to tolerate malaria tablets, Rosemary was hospitalised in Ibadan for over six weeks with cerebral malaria. At the time, educational opportunities for English youngsters in Nigeria ended at the age of eleven. Transition to boarding school in England was the norm, but Amanda's parents rejected that option, so in 1971, a few weeks before giving birth to Adele, Rosemary and the children left Nigeria permanently for Hessle, Yorkshire. Colin returned to England in 1972, at which time the family settled in Gravesend, Kent.

Recalling life in Ewekoro, Amanda described being housed in a small isolated compound in the African bush along with the other English families who made up the site's population. As was typical of the time, each expatriate household was supported by local villagers called stewards. On one hand, the system created employment for the villagers, but on the other, it was not something of which Amanda's parents approved: "It was forced on [the villagers] ... but the stewards did become family friends." Amenities in the compound were few; there was a golf course, which Colin frequented, and a swimming pool. "Everyone socialised around the pool every day. I learned to swim when I was about eighteen months old, taught by my parents, and swam every day for fun."

Going to school required catching a school bus each morning at 6:00 a.m. to travel 64 kilometres to Ikeja, the capital city of Lagos State and the location of the school nearest to Ewekoro. The trip could be unsettling because, during the Biafran War (1967–1970), soldiers armed with rifles searched the bus each day.

The transition to life in England was not without obstacles. Something as seemingly simple as manoeuvring in traffic proved daunting. "I was seven and a bit, and I remember my mom preventing me from going on school trips, which I never understood. But I had no sense of roads and traffic, and she was concerned that the teaching staff might not appreciate that about me. It was a safety thing; it's funny how it sticks in my mind."

Accustomed to a small, isolated, tightknit community, Amanda found integration into English life challenging. For her parents, the solution was to build on the very active outdoor life she had enjoyed in Nigeria and involve her in as many activities as possible: ballet, tap dancing, Latin American dancing, gymnastics, piano, and fatefully, in 1973, swimming at the Gravesend and Northfleet Swimming Club.

Dancing captivated young Amanda. Her ballet teacher, Barbara Fothergill, had danced professionally, and most of the students in her dance class later became professional dancers. When Amanda was twelve, the family moved to the small town of Trowbridge, Wiltshire. There the dance schools lacked the quality she was used to, so swimming became the focus of her quest to excel. When Trowbridge Amateur Swimming Club was unable to offer sufficient pool time for Amanda, a talented backstroker, to progress to higher levels, she joined Street and District Swim Club, 40 miles away in Somerset. The route from home to club covered old twisting country roads and took an hour there and back, so Amanda moved on to the Thamesdown Swimming Club (TSC) in Swindon. "It was still a forty-minute drive, but it was a slightly better club. It meant getting up at four o'clock in the morning to get to training and then going to school afterwards. There were limitations, challenges ... I swam at county, regional, and national meets and I knew that technically I was good and that my parents gave me the best opportunity they could."

As Amanda struggled to find a swim club that would nurture her dreams of excelling, she was encountering educational challenges. A gifted student, she found John of Gaunt School in Trowbridge was ill-suited to her interests and capabilities. "Girls weren't allowed to do woodwork or technical drawing or metal work; they were only allowed cookery and needlework courses, and I wasn't very good at those things. My teachers discouraged me from taking science subjects as they said girls don't need to do science, and I was science oriented. Later, when I decided that I wanted to be a physiotherapist as a backup to coaching — because I didn't think I could earn a livelihood in coaching — I discovered I had done the wrong A-Level subjects, and that became a challenge."

Amanda Booth

Transitioning from Athlete to Coach to Physiotherapist

By September 1982, nineteen-year-old Amanda had realised that her dream of winning swimming medals at the national level was beyond reach. While the TSC coach "was very good, he was unreliable. We'd travel to Swindon to find him still in bed. I was more committed than the coach was; that's why I gave it up."

As difficult as that decision was, Amanda realised she could stay in the sport when she was offered the part-time head coaching job at the nearby Frome Swimming Club (FSC). She had been a volunteer coach at her other clubs and, while she "absolutely loved it," she accepted that coaching was not a paying proposition nor did it seem to be an option as a profession; the most she could expect financially was payment of her expenses. "One reason for later deciding to do the physiotherapy qualification was that I needed to be something else that would allow me to coach."

During her three years with FSC, Amanda gained coaching certificates from the Amateur Swimming Association (now Swim England) and started working as a part-time physiotherapy helper. In 1987, she enrolled in Moray House School of Education and Sport in Edinburgh, which offered the only sports coaching diploma in Britain and included a sports medicine module she hoped would confirm whether physiotherapy was the profession for her. While there, she held a part-time group coach position with the Warrender Baths Club and gained experience doing lactate testing for Scottish Swimming.

Upon completing the course in 1989, Amanda moved to Manchester to begin her studies in physiotherapy at the University of Salford. Her schedule was hectic. She worked fourteen hours a week as a group coach on a temporary contract at the City of Salford Swimming Club (CSSC) with two early morning sessions and another at 6:00 p.m. Her physio studies ran from nine to five on weekdays. Hospital placements had to be managed when the course wasn't in session, and she negotiated these to take place in Manchester or nearby. In 1991, she was awarded the chartered physiotherapist designation.

Amanda spent the next five years working full time for the National Health Service (NHS) and continued her fourteen hours of coaching, an integral part of her life. Given a squad of twelve underrated swimmers, she decided that they were in fact talented and set out to prove it.

She still did not view coaching as a career, given that women were mostly limited to being part-time swimming teachers. Working with people and building relationships are common to both coaching and physiotherapy and explain Amanda's attraction to the professions. "Coaching was something I wanted to do, and I just got on with it. I'm very much a carer, a helper ... helping others to achieve their full potential is something I've always enjoyed. From experiences I've had, I know that many people with ability do not necessarily get the right person to nurture them."

As for the underrated CSSC swimmers, before long, all twelve went to the national championships, four became international swimmers, and one, Nicole Thornley, competed at the 1992 European Junior Championships and the 1994 Commonwealth Games. "After I developed swimmers who had been written off by the other coaches, the male head coach wanted them to progress to him, but they didn't want to move from me. My contract with CSSC was terminated, I did a professional handover and left to concentrate on my physio career."

In 1996, Amanda became a locum physiotherapist, which gave her career flexibility and allowed her to complete a postgraduate diploma in academic and practical physiotherapy from Queen Mary University of London; in 1997, she earned a diploma in sports massage from the National Sports Medicine Institute. After leaving the CSSC, she had moved to Birmingham and worked at a private sports clinic in a local hospital. Eventually, she decided to leave the NHS, having reached the point where career and financial progression would entail moving into management, an unpalatable option given her preference for working with people instead of administration. Her interest in treating sport injuries took her to Cardiff, Wales, and the Welsh Institute of Sport where she was instrumental in establishing its physiotherapy clinic. As the physiotherapist for the British swimming and triathlon teams at international meets and World Cups, her resume and her reputation grew.

Making Difficult Choices

By 1999, Amanda was on the English list to go to the 2000 Olympic Games in Sydney, Australia, as a physiotherapist. Leading up to the Games, she travelled to Australia to attend a six-week training camp for the senior swimming team. Coincidentally, Ian Turner, then the head of British Swimming, asked her to apply for the age and youth swimming coach position at the British Swimming Performance Centre in Bath. It was a dilemma: an Olympic opportunity as a physiotherapist versus a return to coaching. "I couldn't do both, and I chose coaching ... it was my first full-time coaching job, and I accepted even though it meant a salary cut and paid less than my physiotherapy income, so I continued with part-time physiotherapy work."

One of Amanda's many innovations was arranging boarding at a local residential school for four elite athletes who lived too far from the facility to travel there each day. This allowed them to train full time in her programme; each went on to make British teams.

During her time at Bath, Amanda was mentored by Bill Sweetman, British Swimming's national performance director, who provided coach education. He and national youth coach John Atkinson gave her the opportunity to head British Swimming's World Class Start programmes, national camps that identify, develop, and support talented swimmers as they pursue international success.

Eventually, another difficult decision loomed. In 2002, Amanda and fellow swim coach Jon Rudd[21] married. He was coaching at Plymouth Leander Swimming Club (PLSC), around 230 kilometres southwest of Bath. The question was, Which of the two would move? Amanda had built up a reputation in Bath; also, it has a 50-metre facility and was the first national swimming centre. Rudd had only seven national-level swimmers at PLSC and was working at a state school in Plymouth.

Amanda opted to move to Plymouth when an opportunity arose for PLSC to go into partnership with Plymouth College, an independent school that had its own pool onsite. This meant that PLSC could be based at the college and have exclusive use of its five-lane, 25-metre pool outside of school hours. It also gave Amanda the opportunity to develop a boarding model as she had done in Bath.

---

[21] As the performance director of Irish Swimming, Rudd coached Ruta Meilutyte of Lithuania, the 100-metre breaststroke gold medallist at the 2012 Olympic Games, and sprinter Ben Proud, the world and Commonwealth champion from England. He is the president of the World Swimming Coaches Association.

Five years after establishing the link between PLSC and the college, Jon was appointed the college's director of swimming. Together, Amanda and Jon went on to further develop its programme, which started with only a few boarders and eventually offered thirty-two places for boarders. Amanda also continued working part time as a physiotherapist with the English Institute of Sport, focusing on diving and weightlifting.

With the births of George in 2002 and Jack in 2004, Amanda adjusted her priorities while maintaining her commitment to coaching. She returned three days after giving birth to George but focused on local programmes to be closer to home. She had established a private physio clinic in her home and had a physio room at the college. She also had a part-time contract with the English Institute of Sport, working mainly with British Diving's four international divers. Making all this possible was a strong support network that included swimmers' parents — but especially Amanda's parents. "My mom has been very much involved in helping to support me, and my dad has always been there." Amanda recorded numerous coaching successes during this period; one of her proudest achievements is coaching Achieng Ajulu-Bushell[22] from the age of fourteen to becoming British champion at sixteen and the first Black woman to swim for Britain at the European Aquatics Championships.

In 2010, first separated and then divorced, Amanda decided to move on to become the head coach of the City of Oxford Swimming Club (COSC), a club with only two swimmers who had posted national qualifying times.

Over the next ten years, under Amanda's leadership, the COSC achieved more success than at any other time in its history, winning the overall trophy at Oxfordshire North Bucks County Championships for eight consecutive years, making the National Arena Swimming League finals for six consecutive years, and in 2019,

---

[22] Melina Spanoudi, "Canongate Acquires Debut by Ex-Team GB Swimmer Ajulu-Bushell," *The Bookseller*, April 28, 2023, https://www.thebookseller.com/rights/canongate-acquires-debut-by-ex-team-gb-swimmer-ajulu-bushell.

bringing thirty-three swimmers to the national championships. Six swimmers competed internationally for teams from England, Scotland, Wales, and Great Britain; and David Murphy and Nick Skelton were multiple medallists. By 2020, the COSC had sixty-six national qualifiers.

In 2016, Amanda was one of fifteen coaches selected for the 2017 cohort of Swim England's Coach 2024 programme, "an intensive fourteen-month learning journey for coaches who aspire to excellence and coaching at world-class levels." The programme included workshops and international coaching opportunities and enabled coaches to share experiences, skills, and knowledge. Through this programme, Amanda worked with coaching mentors Emma Mitchell, performance lifestyle coach for Great Britain Hockey, and Joanna Jones, course leader of Coach 2024 at the time. Both women challenged and encouraged her to reflect on her own coaching practice. "I developed better links with other coaches and with the Swim England staff, and that was invaluable." She was also appointed to numerous national and international camps and teams as head coach, including the 2017 Commonwealth Youth Games in Bahamas and the 2020 FFN Golden Tour Nice International Meet.

Throughout Amanda's tenure with the COSC, her parents continued to be stalwart in their support. "It has been hard to bring up two boys on my own. My mother lives nearly seventy miles away and has stayed three to four nights each week because I needed someone at home so I could coach early morning practices. My dad has always been there, especially not complaining when my mom stayed over."

Jack's diagnoses of autistic spectrum disorder, sensory processing disorder, and attention deficit hyperactivity disorder brought new challenges, but Amanda saw this as an opportunity to gain an understanding of different learning styles and the various ways children process information. "This has had a big impact on my coaching style. My son had problems with fine motor skills, proprioception (the sense of self-movement, force, and body position), and spatial awareness. Using my physiotherapy knowledge,

I worked on increasing proprioception and developing movement patterns on poolside (land) and progressed this awareness into development drills in the pool. This land-to-pool transfer work has helped the kinaesthetic learners but also swimmers who have proprioceptive awareness issues."

Experiencing the Women Coach Internship Programme

A significant outcome of Amanda's selection to the WCIP was hearing nineteen "incredible" stories from the other interns. "Even now I get a little bit of a lump, get quite emotional. Their stories resonated so much as did their struggles, which are so like what I have experienced. They made me reflect on things I had bottled up and coped with in my own way. I never really discussed those problems and experiences; I had a stiff upper lip and got on with it. [The stories] have made me very sensitive to other coaches and what they experience as women coaches.

"I think that was the first time I evaluated what a difficult struggle coaching is, not just for me, but for so many other women. WCIP helped me to reflect and have a greater understanding of my own journey and the challenges I've faced ... it was empowering to find I was not alone."

Facing Challenges as Women Coaches

As Amanda reflected on the early years of her coaching career, she opined that, back then, women were probably more accepting of certain situations than they would be nowadays. "There were challenges for women in many aspects of life ... I didn't see swimming as being different. Culturally, that's how things were and, awful to say, most male coaches were having relationships with their female swimmers, which now would be really frowned upon. When I went to national conferences, it was assumed that the only way a woman coach could progress was to sleep with a male coach. Sounds awful, doesn't it, but that's what was happening at the time.

"I wanted to be respected; I was only seventeen when I went to my first national conference, and I remember what a challenge it was to get people to take me seriously."

Another attitudinal challenge was countering the viewpoint that coaching wasn't a "proper" job. Most of Amanda's school friends went on to university and considered her involvement to be odd. "Their attitude was, 'Coaching's not going to take you anywhere. Why are you wasting your time doing this?' It made me determined to prove them wrong."

As a divorced mother of two teenage boys, Amanda had to balance looking after them while building her coaching career, not to mention trying — and failing — to find time for herself. "Some judge that I cannot be fully committed or as successful as a coach because I am a mother, an attitude which can be frustrating. All I need is understanding of my circumstances and being given sufficient time to organise and prepare in advance."

In her experience, which is common to numerous women coaches, male coaches have taken credit for her ideas. Even worse, having a successful swimmer has been attributed to the swimmer's talent and Amanda's "luck" rather than to her having done a good job.

Amanda Booth(centre) was part of the Swim England coaching staff at the 2017 Commonwealth Youth Games in Bahamas.

Challenged by COVID and COSC

The COVID-19 pandemic created substantial challenges for Amanda, some of a surprising nature as they emanated from the COSC. During the first lockdown, which ran from March 23 to May 10, 2020, she was able to communicate with all the club's swimmers and coaching staff. She and Matt Croyle (strength and conditioning coach) ran educational sessions and technique workshops over Zoom for the COSC and several other clubs, and both were paid a full-time salary.

During the second lockdown, from November 5 to December 2, 2020, Amanda was on part-time furlough whereby the government paid 80 per cent of her salary but she was not allowed to work.

Come the third lockdown — from January 6 to March 8, 2021 — Amanda was put on full-time flexible furlough. "This means the club would pay my salary and could claim 80 per cent back. It was optional whether the club paid me the other 20 per cent, which they did not. I was allowed two hours a week to keep in contact with my top squad. Only part-time work was available. The scheme allowed sport clubs to function even as they furloughed their staffs."

At that point, Amanda's problems with the COSC escalated. When she had first arrived at the club, she was the only professional coach; that number had grown to five. The club is administered by a committee of parent volunteers, and they made the decision to furlough Amanda and the other coaches. Further actions by the committee left her feeling unsettled.

"It was time to evaluate what is important. Do I continue to coach? Do I focus on coach mentoring or education/tutoring? Do I return to physiotherapy? The furlough affected my profile and silenced my voice as head coach, influencing the balance within the club and allowing it to become committee-led rather than coach-led."

Amanda feels that one source of the problem is the general attitude in Britain towards coaching as a profession. "It is not necessarily respected. If I say I am a physiotherapist, I get a lot more respect than if I say I'm a coach. People may say, 'But what's your proper job?' I hope that somehow, we can change that in the future."

On Being Upended

In April 2021, the COSC coaching staff resigned en masse. In a message to their swimmers, the coaches — Amanda, Matt, Mikey Hire, Zichen Liu, and Fabian Whitbread — stated that they were "no longer in a position to deliver the coach-led, athlete-centred, and committee-supported programme [they] all desired to be a part of." Accusations and counteraccusations ensued, and since December 2022, Amanda has been waiting for an employment tribunal (to occur in March 2024).[23]

For now, Amanda has put her coaching career on hold since there are no other performance coaching jobs in the Oxford area, and her son Jack needs to remain in the Oxford school system with its excellent autism programmes in junior and secondary school. Financially strapped after the resignation, Amanda credited the support of her parents and immediate family with making it possible for her to stay put. She resumed physiotherapy with the NHS, has continued as a coach developer for Swim England, and is a tutor for the Senior Coach qualification. In April 2022, she assumed a part-time position as director of swimming for the Portsmouth Northsea Swimming Club. When Jack completes his A-Levels in June 2023, she hopes to move to Portsmouth and further develop this new role.

More good news: Amanda was selected by Mel Marshall, the celebrated British coach of Olympic and world champion Adam Peaty, to support British Swimming's relay programme. She has also joined the British Swimming Coaches Association management board, working to support coaches. "I remain optimistic that good comes from all of the challenges we face."

---

23 "Review Clears Former COSC Coaches of Any Safeguarding Concerns," British Swimming Coaches Association, June 12, 2021,
https://www.gbswimcoaches.co.uk/news/2021/review-clears-former-cosc-coaches-of-any-safeguarding-concerns.

Chapter Nine

Cordelia Norris

New Zealand

When toddler Cordelia Norris first dove into her family's backyard pool in Auckland, New Zealand, her family could never have imagined her having a professional career as one of their country's top diving coaches. Little did she know that within days of her twentieth birthday she would be coaching New Zealand's elite divers at the 2018 Commonwealth Games in Gold Coast, Australia.

Energetic, fearless, cheeky, clever, committed, and *driven*: These words capture young Cordelia's personality. A perfectionist who expected a lot of herself, athletically and academically, she has always enjoyed developing relationships with people she respects and who she aspired to please. "I handed homework in on time and worked hard to achieve the best possible grades, especially in classes where I developed a rapport with the teacher." She also had a prankish side, she said, recalling with a laugh being scolded by a teacher for climbing the doorframe of her classroom.

Cordelia was born to Andrew, an accountant, and full-time mom Diane on April 14, 1998, in Auckland, and has two younger siblings, Honor and Callum. A close-knit family, the five frequently enjoyed holidays together, most often at Lake Taupō, New Zealand's largest lake, in the central North Island, where they had a holiday house. "I loved it there and have many fond memories of the family all being together. Dad would take us out on the boat, and we fished, water-skied, wakeboarded, and enjoyed the 'biscuit,' an inflatable inner tube he towed behind the boat. He would take us to what we called 'our rocks' in a secluded bay accessible only by boat where we jumped into the crystal-clear water. When we weren't on the boat, we enjoyed family walks and bike rides." At home, she was in constant motion, climbing, doing cartwheels, and jumping on the backyard trampoline.

From the age of two, Cordelia attended an academically focused preschool, which encouraged early reading and writing. This gave her a head start when she entered Greenhithe Primary School as a five-year-old. The school was a five-minute walk from the family home. Its motto is "Ko te piko o te māhuri, tērā te tupu o te rākau," which means "The way the sapling is shaped determines how the tree grows." Physical activity was built into each school day, including JUMP JAM[24] lessons, physical education, outdoor education, and sports.

---

[24] "JUMP JAM is a 'Kidz Aerobix' resource kit created by Brett Fairweather specifically for aged 6 to 12 years old + teachers to challenge fundamental movements skills, increase fitness, develop student leadership and motivate students to move & enjoy exercise."— From jumpjam.co.nz on September 19, 2023.

Cordelia Norris

However much Cordelia enjoyed being active, scholastic achievement was of prime importance. "In primary school, if Mum felt I wasn't getting enough homework, she'd set me more. I remember sitting at the kitchen bench completing maths sheets she had printed out for me and Honor. Callum was only a baby…"

Chores were part of daily life, with Cordelia assigned to empty the dishwasher and do odd jobs, such as washing the car, for which she was paid $10, and picking up fallen leaves for $1. Later on she was expected to cook dinner one night a week, clean the bathrooms and her bedroom, tidy up the house, and unload the car upon arrival at Taupō.

Driven to Excel

Cordelia started swimming lessons as a two-year-old, mainly from necessity, New Zealand being surrounded by the Pacific Ocean and the Tasman Sea. Once she became proficient enough to swim laps, boredom set in, and she asked to stop. "I love the water, but just swimming and doing strokes was really monotonous!"

Given Auckland's temperate climate, Cordelia spent much of her free time diving off the side of her backyard swimming pool, an activity she began as a five-year-old. When she reached the age of ten, Diane suggested diving lessons, and she agreed. "That was when I got the courage. I don't really know what the attraction was; I like flipping and being acrobatic, I love the water, and I was okay with heights so I thought diving would be a cool thing to do."

Cordelia also played football and tennis, excelling at both. However, as with swimming, their appeal faded. With tennis, she tired of playing long games under the hot sun. And getting hit in the head and stomach with a football was so traumatising that she became a "very cautious" player. By the age of twelve, she decided to dedicate herself to diving.

Enjoyment of the sport was as important to Cordelia as getting results. Training with the North Harbour Diving club, she resolved to progress as far as she could and quickly posted promising scores. In 2010, she beat a competitive field to win gold in the 1-metre springboard in her age group at the Autumn Championships. She went on to represent New Zealand at the junior level and competed at several small international competitions in Australia as well as the 2011 Asia Pacific Rim Diving Championships in Wellington, New Zealand, where she won the bronze medal on the 3-metre springboard knockout event for fourteen- and fifteen-year-old girls.

Although homework, studying, and diving consumed much of Cordelia's after-school time, friendships were always important. "I had a great group of school friends, and I was really close to those I did sport with. The divers I trained with are still some of the people closest to me. We've shared the ups and downs of the sport and life together. Winning, losing…"

Between diving and attending Albany Senior High School, Cordelia followed a gruelling schedule, studying in every spare moment: on the school bus, during lunch break, in the car on the way to diving practice. "I had always done well at school and wanted to keep that up. Our marks are graded Achieved, Merit, and Excellence, and I wanted Excellence! My last year was insane, and I was studying a lot, but it paid off as I got Highest Achievement Academic in 2015, my graduating year."

Earlier, Cordelia felt compelled to make a choice and, at the end of 2014, when she was sixteen years old, she retired from diving. She had been competing on both springboard and tower, the latter becoming increasingly frightening. "It was a culmination of things. It's a terrifying sport; it's the heights and doing flips off the tower; I was sick of the stress of constantly being scared. My coach and I didn't have a great understanding of each other, so I decided to end it."

Almost immediately Cordelia found herself coaching, although not exactly by choice. Liam Stone, now one of New Zealand's best divers, was one of her clubmates, and his father, Lindsay, was both the coach and a family friend. On the heels of her retirement, Lindsay dropped by her house to tell her he needed her help coaching one of his classes at a holiday camp. Scared, she turned him down because she had never coached. But she found out, he is stubborn. "And so there I was, on the deck and coaching."

It wasn't as though Cordelia intended coaching to be her career; medicine was her goal. New Zealand requires aspiring doctors to complete one year of biomedical science, after which the best prospects for medical school are selected. Cordelia's decision to pursue medicine was last minute and not well thought out. "I ignored the fact that I have a phobia of hospitals." After a half semester, she found herself in a bad place. "I wanted to be the best I could be in each area of my life, that is, university and coaching, but there wasn't any maintainable and healthy way for me to do both successfully. When Steve Gladding, lead, Coach Development Pathway, Diving New Zealand (DNZ) suggested coaching could be a career, I responded, 'Really?' But coaching became my escape from biomedicine and all my struggles. Steve had thought that one day I could become the team doctor, but when he realised what a bad place I was in, he offered me a part-time coaching job ... Maybe he knew me better than I knew myself."

Being in a "Horrible Place"

By the age of eighteen, Cordelia's lifestyle had become neither manageable nor maintainable. She described a typical day:

"I woke up early, ate breakfast, and caught the bus to the university for an eight a.m. lab that ran until noon. I would run straight to a lecture and then had a one-hour break, which I used to work out at the gym, leaving me no time for lunch — I'd eat carrot sticks instead of a proper lunch and so wasn't fuelling myself well. Next came back-to-back lectures for three to four hours.

"Everything was just so fast — information, information, information — and there was no time to process all that information; I felt so overwhelmed because I like to really understand things.

"I thought, this is the rest of my life; I don't have a way out. I felt quite depressed and got physically sick from the stress.

"After classes, I would go straight to the pool — I was always late; another stress — and coach for two hours and then get a ride home with Lindsay Stone. By then it was nine p.m.

"I remember Steve having a word with me because I was eating instant coffee straight out of a packet; it tasted terrible, but I had to stay awake.

"It was not a good way to live, trying to do school and coach. I remember being on the bus and it felt like I had just run a marathon. My family and friends knew I was busy, but I never let on how much I was struggling. I really trusted Steve, so eventually I opened up to him."

In Cordelia's world, coaching was not considered a particularly desirable profession, and so initially she wavered, having enrolled for the second semester of biomedicine. The day classes were set to begin, she made her decision. Coaching won out.

While Cordelia's parents were understanding, they weren't

certain that coaching diving, a small sport in New Zealand that didn't pay well, could really be a career. Still, they were happy that she would no longer be "in that horrible place" and that she was focusing on something she loved. "They really supported me."

Creating a Coaching Career

As Cordelia helped Steve to coach the twenty divers on the competitive squad and in the beginner and recreational classes, she was coming to see the feasibility of a coaching career. "It was a bit scary because my life had been in an academic setting, but I knew that leaving the medical pathway was the right decision." It helped that Steve created an equitable environment. Together they planned the season and the training sessions and alternated coaching tower and springboard. He dedicated a substantial amount of time to constructing resources that enabled her to be successful as a person and as a coach. "I definitely would be nowhere near where I am if it wasn't for Steve. Mentorship is crucial for coach development."

To hone her coaching skills, in 2017, Cordelia began an undergraduate bachelor of science degree majoring in psychology at Massey University. "It makes good sense for a coach. It was hard work, but it's much more holistic [than medicine] and it fits me better as a person. I chose to do it through correspondence because of my variable coaching hours and time away at competitions."

It was Steve who persuaded Cordelia to apply for the WCIP. Her first reaction was, "I'm not ready for this!" But he persisted and she was accepted, the youngest of the group of twenty. (She celebrated her twentieth birthday during the Games.) The internship was a direct extension of her role with DNZ, coaching athletes to achieve their international potential. Steve continued to mentor her at the Games and structured a programme that increased her knowledge, experience, and personal development and replicated their domestic roles, including assisting with warm-ups, conditioning, dryland and pre-competition practices, and involvement during competition and briefing and debriefing sessions.

"The WCIP was a fantastic initiative, one of the best things I've been involved in. Often, we are led to develop our coaching in technical courses run by men in our discipline. The WCIP was a multidisciplinary group led by women, for women coaches. The range of different sports broadened my understanding of sport and not only what it takes to be a successful coach but to be a successful leader and mentor. Attending the WCIP gave me further opportunities in my coaching; it gave me a group of women whom I can use as a sounding board, who support each other and bounce off each other to grow. This is an essential aspect of keeping women coaches in sport."

Post-WCIP, Cordelia's coaching career blossomed. She took two divers to Montréal, Canada, for the 2018 CAMO Invitational competition, the first time on her own as a coach. She was selected as a coach for the 2018 Youth Olympic Games in Buenos Aires, Argentina; although her athletes missed out on selection, the nomination was "a great honour."

In 2020, Steve, "feeling he had done his time," stepped away from active coaching to focus on managing Auckland Diving's programme, and Cordelia became the club's performance coach. She explained that Steve's family commitments made it difficult to manage all the travelling required of the role. His passion had shifted to growing and developing the sport in New Zealand rather than focusing on the few athletes at the top.

Cordelia relishes her new role: "I coach seven divers, and it's a lot more responsibility; it's also more gratifying. You can really get to know each of them. With all the training they do, they spend more time with me than with friends and family, so I don't take lightly the influence I have on them. It can be challenging when I must make tough calls, which Steve and I used to do together; now all that responsibility falls on me."

Coach Cordelia Norris and diver Liam Stone are happy with his performance at the 2023 World Cup series in Xi'an, China.

The COVID-19 Challenge

The New Zealand government reacted swiftly to COVID-19. In late February 2020, the country's borders were closed and lockdown restrictions imposed. A state of national emergency was declared from March 25 to May 13, 2020. There was a second lockdown during August and September 2020 and a third in February and March 2021. From August until December 3, 2021, Auckland remained in a form of lockdown until border restrictions, public gathering limits, and vaccine mandate requirements were eased between February and May 2022. In September 2022, the government lifted the remaining vaccine mandates and mask requirements.

Because she is an introvert, the first lockdown didn't trouble Cordelia, who initially enjoyed the slower pace and extra time at home. She and Steve were still job-sharing and held daily Zoom calls with the divers, and she connected with her close friends through social media and video calls and continued studying through correspondence. It was a different matter for the divers, who struggled with the isolation of training alone. "Honestly, the lockdowns were such a blur, but the divers were away from the pool for far too long. In some cases, even when we were no longer in a strict lockdown, the pools remained closed. We ran dryland sessions in my backyard, as I have a trampoline, did strength and conditioning at the beach, and went to the local wharf for dive training.

"The pool closures slowed our progress, but it was a time the divers will never forget. It forced us to be creative in our training as we kept them bonded as a team."

When the coaches managed to arrange domestic competitions and regional events, the divers were excited and motivated. At the end of 2020, for example, a virtual online event provided the Kiwis with a safe and unique competitive option involving Japan, Malaysia, New Zealand, Australia, and Singapore. Each pool set up a camera to film each dive; the judges scored from their homes with the results displayed as usual on a scoreboard. "An animated arrow zoomed into our pool signalling when it was our turn to dive. It was awesome!"

Throughout the lockdowns, Cordelia continued to plan as though major championships would proceed, tracking the divers' skill levels, mobility, and strength and conditioning, and setting appropriate goals for each so that they would be ready when restrictions were lifted. Long term, she aims to coach New Zealand divers at an Olympic Games. "[Now] is the strongest position DNZ has been in, with potential Olympians in contention. It's about the journey we are taking together; that's the important part. We start with long-term planning, so we know what we are aiming for and then I work backwards. For each year, I figure out what skills they should have and what events they need to attend to be on track. I then break things down into different phases for each season, including an off-season, where they improve their fitness and work on the basics, and the competitive season.

"Coaching is mostly about helping athletes achieve their goals, so my working life revolves around them. I don't make goals for myself, because so many factors are out of my control: whether my athletes are selected for the team, how they compete on the day, who their competition is, if I am selected to coach at the event. So, for myself, I focus on the process and the journey. I know that if I've done everything possible to help them achieve their goal, I'm doing my job well."

On Being Dealt a Sudden and Hard Blow

In September 2020, Cordelia began to experience pain, first in her hands and then in her shoulder, pelvis, and neck. Initially, she put the pain down to a traumatic event when a parent came to poolside while she was coaching and behaved aggressively. Frightened, she fainted, hitting her head. A subsequent court hearing was upsetting, overwhelming, and had a negative impact on her mental health. Cordelia assumed the pain was her body reacting to the situation. Her physiotherapist, Patrick Peng, an ex-gymnast and Commonwealth Games competitor, thought otherwise and insisted that she consult her general practitioner, which she did in February 2021. By this time, the pain was affecting her entire body. She couldn't walk well and was limping; in the mornings, her hands were so painful that she couldn't grip her car's steering wheel; some days her shoulders hurt so much that even a slight movement of her arm was agonising.

An urgent referral to a rheumatologist resulted in a diagnosis of rheumatoid arthritis (RA) on March 8, 2021. "It felt like my life had been flipped upside down. I struggled to comprehend my diagnosis and what this disease meant for me. Everyone was very supportive and helped me through one of the darkest times of my life ... there was a ninety per cent chance I would be on drugs for the rest of my life. The drug they started me on is very potent and left me feeling nauseous, fatigued, and experiencing brain fog. I knew this is only the beginning of a lifelong journey."

Cordelia refused to let RA rule her life. She graduated from university and eagerly resumed travelling to competitions as head coach, including the 2022 World Aquatics Championships in Budapest, Hungary, in June; the Bolzano Diving Meet in July; the 2022 Commonwealth Games in Birmingham, England, also in July;

and the FINA World Junior Diving Championships in Montréal, Canada, in November.

Importantly, her disease has become relatively stable, the dosage of the drug that caused such unpleasant side effects has been lowered significantly, and she has been approved for a new kind of medicine called biologics. "This has improved my quality of life, as the new drugs are working well and have minimal side effects."

Looking ahead, Cordelia's focus is building towards qualification for the Paris 2024 Olympic Games. "Regardless of the outcome, I know my athletes and I are on a big journey together, filled with travelling, laughter, love, hard work, highs and lows. To relax, I go on bike rides with my dad and walk the dog with my mom. I still love the trampoline and spend a lot of time on it in summer. And I am still a very keen photographer."

Note: A gifted photographer, Cordelia's works are attracting attention for their originality and beauty. You can look up her work at Cordelia Norris Photography, https://www.facebook.com/people/Cordelia-Norris-Photography/100075627116906/.

Chapter Ten

Carolyne Anyango Kola

Kenya

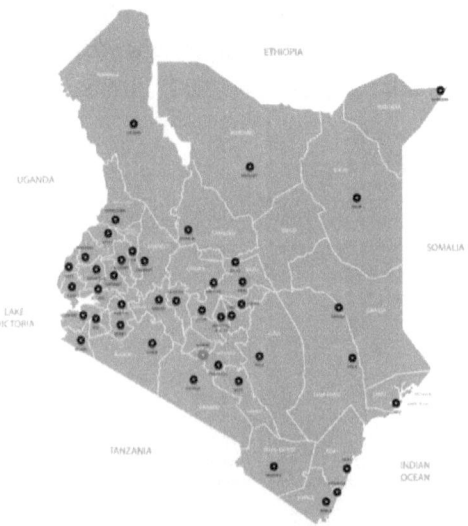

Siaya County in the former Nyanza Province of Kenya is far from the playing fields of international sport and has not produced any of the legendary Kenyan distance runners. It is, however, the birthplace of Carolyne Anyango Kola, one of the country's most accomplished decathletes of the 1990s and now a leading coach of its Paralympic and Deaf athletes.

Born on May 5, 1960, to Jessica Awuor and George Samuel Ochola, Carolyne was the fifth-born in a family of eight girls and five boys. Her father, a civil engineer with East African Railways Corporation (EARC), worked five days a week in Nakuru, a city in the Rift Valley region some 240 kilometres from Siaya County where her mother, whom Carolyne described as "a strong lady and an excellent netball player," raised her children and worked for the corporation as teacher at Nyalenda Railways Nursery School.

In 1967, George was transferred to Kisumu, a leading economic centre on the edge of Lake Victoria. The whole family followed him to a corporate housing estate his employer provided for their workers. "It was like a family. Apart from school, the estate was self-contained and included a well-provisioned shopping centre with a market that offered a wide variety of foodstuffs, most of which was grown locally. In the town itself, many locals made their living running small-scale businesses and working in agriculture, with the primary crops being maize, groundnuts, beans, and sorghum."

Prior to the move, Carolyne attended Bondeni Primary School in Nakuru, which was within walking distance of her home. Entering Lower Primary at the age of five, she was in the same class as her brother Isaac, who was close in age to her and acted as her protector. School started at eight o'clock in the morning and the children rushed home for lunch and then headed back to school until two. Evening play included running with bottles on top of their heads and competitions involving hopping while wearing sacks.

All the Ochola children were expected to contribute to running the household, with everyone doing the domestic work. "In my mother's house, each of us had a task; mine was washing dishes and preparing food for my siblings. I was always advised that, as a girl, I had to learn all the housekeeping chores; having gained experience from the assigned duties really helped me when I grew up."

Fortunately for Carolyne, EARC encouraged unstructured sports on the estate. On weekends, children played various traditional games, which Carolyne credited with helping to shape her later sports career. These included hide-and-seek; marbles (banta), which is often played with nuts, seeds, stones, or dried fruits; rolling old bicycle tyres; dolls made from old pieces of clothes and wood; and soccer, the most common game for Kenyan children, often played with balls made from rolling plastic bags and tying them together with ropes.

While in nursery school, Carolyne had discovered a "very aggressive" side to her personality, which manifested itself in never wanting to lose, a trait that was honed during her later athletic career and which continues to this day. Eventually, she followed her mother into netball, it being "the sport for girls." Although the estate lacked much in the way of facilities, there was a netball ground, and Jessica remained a valued member of the corporation's team even after she married and had children.

Carolyne Anyango Kola

In 1978, upon completion of Fourth Form, the final year of secondary school, and having earned her O-Levels, Carolyne took a job with the Municipal Council of Kisumu as a junior clerk and joined its netball team, playing goal defence and goal shooter. She competed at the East and Central African Netball Championships in Zimbabwe and won five titles at the Inter-Council Games before retiring in 1986. "My mum was my mentor; she actively encouraged me to compete in netball although she didn't set a goal for me. I used to watch her and admired the way she played."

Several of Carolyne's siblings were also involved in athletics and netball. Her younger sister Risper Akumu could, Carolyne said, have been much better than her but wasn't keen on training. Her younger brother Isaac Ochola was talented, but his career was cut short through injury. Another younger sister, Lydia Akinyi, became Carolyne's rival: "Whatever I did, she wanted to do too. When we were older, and I was employed by Kenya Posts and Telecommunications (KPT) and she for the EARC, there were intercorporation competitions and we competed in high jump; sometimes she won, and sometimes I did."

A Talented Late Bloomer

In 1982, at the age of twenty-two, Carolyne joined KPT in Kisumu as an employee and player on its netball team. Shortly thereafter, she was transferred 340 kilometres away to Nairobi, where most of the other players were based. "At first it was difficult because I was used to Kisumu, but I had to go because it was employment, and the teammates and coaches were very good. Around that time, I formally started athletics since KPT also had a track and field team."

It marked the beginning of what would be an illustrious career as a heptathlete that would take her to many of the world's most prestigious competitions, including the Commonwealth Games. At the time, team manager Francis Paul encouraged her to get involved in heptathlon, about which she knew nothing. "I thought that maybe he saw something in me that no one else had, so I just went ahead, and it is by the grace of God that I did it."

To call this unusual is an understatement. Two years earlier, twenty-year-old Carolyne had married Ezekial Otieno Kola and in short order gave birth to three sons: Noel Owuor, Maxwell Vincent, and John Dickens Onyang'o. The couple had met at All Saints' Cathedral where both were members of the choir. Ezekial, who worked as a researcher with the Ministry of Agriculture in Kisumu, also moved to Nairobi. The children were still young and, as Caroylne noted, still needed "motherly care."

Doing Kenya Proud

By 1987, Carolyne was a skilled heptathlete and ready for international competition. Debuting for Kenya at the All-Africa Games, she finished sixth out of fourteen competitors. She continued with the KPT netball team, and in 1988, playing goal defence, won the gold medal at the East and Central African Netball Championships in Zanzibar, the first Kenyan team to do so. Later that year, she was named to the national team for the East and Central Africa Senior Challenge Cup where Uganda edged Kenya for top spot. The final score of 28–29 was so painful for Carolyne that she quit netball. "It was devastating because the goal shooter only made two shots. The player in that position is supposed to give her all for the team and I felt that she had let us down, that team play wasn't working for me, that I was blaming her [for the loss]. So I decided to concentrate on athletics; if things go wrong, I can blame myself. At least now I owned my events; if I'm defeated, if it's a bad day, it's only me to blame and not anyone else."

As Carolyne grew ever more proficient as a heptathlete, her feelings of pride in her accomplishments grew. "I was so proud; wearing your national colours brings feelings words cannot describe. I have always been my family's celebrity. John Ezekial always said to me after an event: 'Mum, I saw you on TV.'"

As well as being Carolyne's number one supporter, her husband made her athletics career possible by looking after their sons when she travelled to competitions. "My husband and sons were supportive because they also loved sports." She also had an excellent nanny, Dorcas Mbone, who is still a friend today.

In 1991, Carolyne posted a strong fourth-place finish in heptathlon at the Fifth All-African Games in Cairo, Egypt. The following year, she won the silver medal at the African Senior Athletics Championships in Mauritius, edged only by Chrisna Oosthuizen of South Africa. At the 1993 edition of the event, in Durban, South Africa, she contributed to Kenya's seventeen medals and third-place finish overall, winning the bronze medal. Oosthuizen again won gold and fellow South African Maralize Visser took silver.

Next on Carolyne's competitive agenda was the 1994 Commonwealth Games in Victoria, Canada. Her high — and realistic — hopes for a medal were dashed, although her eighth-place finish established a new national record, which still stands as of July 2023. After the team landed in Victoria, the athletics coach, the late Henry Oluoch, promptly vanished, presumably sightseeing according to Carolyne, who was forced to train on her own until the arrival of physiotherapist Thomas Mwololo, who stepped in to support her. "I was strong but naïve and unsure of how to go about training for my first international meeting outside of Africa. I needed guidance; you can't do the heptathlon alone." However disappointing for Carolyne, the experience taught her an important lesson that she later applied to her coaching. "As a coach, you must be there for your athletes. I felt disadvantaged and I hurt my elbow because I was throwing the javelin incorrectly, and he wasn't there to correct me."

Things were different at the 1995 All-Africa Games in Harare, Zimbabwe. The late Cornelius Korir had been assigned as her coach and guided her throughout the Games. When she won the bronze medal, she dedicated it to him. In 1996, at the African Senior Athletics Championships in Yaoundé, Cameroon, she won the gold medal, setting the stage for the upcoming Olympic Games in Atlanta, Georgia. It was while training at a residential camp that Carolyne learned she had lost her spot on the Kenyan team. It was devastating news. Her preparation had been perfect; she was more mature than in Victoria; Coach Cornelius was guiding her; she had improved in long jump, hurdles, and shot put; she was in top form; and she expected to break her own national record.

What happened to Carolyne was not unusual in Kenya at that time. She had been listed as a member of the Olympic team and a ticket had been issued in her name. This did not prevent another person from claiming her ticket; in this case, it was the team manager's wife. As a lesser-known athlete, Carolyne had no protection from such behaviour, nor was help available from the National Olympic Committee of Kenya (NOCK) or the Kenyan Track and Field Federation (now Athletics Kenya). Only later did she learn that she could have simply gone to the airport to pick up her ticket, but that information came too late. Ironically, when the team manager showed up at the airport, he was dropped from the team by Chef de Mission Kipchoge Keino — just retribution, but no solace for Carolyne.

Carolyne's international competitive career ended two years later at the Commonwealth Games in Kuala Lumpur, Malaysia. She pulled a muscle during the high jump, forcing her to quit the competition. "I was old; I was thirty-eight, but I competed nationally until I was forty-one, when I broke the national high jump record."

Beginning Her Coaching Journey

Growing up, Carolyne dreamt of becoming an investigative police officer. When she was hired as a junior clerk by the Municipal Council of Kisumu, that dream faded because she was married and had a job. "Once you had a government job, you settled, and so I focused on my family, my job, and my athletic career."

Much later, in 2003 and in the twilight of her competitive career, Carolyne was training at the AADC Training Centre at the Moi International Stadium in Nairobi when the centre's deputy director, the late Philip Ndoo, a 10,000-metre runner during the 1970s, suggested that she consider venturing into coaching, building on her experience as a demonstrator for coaches taking Level 2 coaching courses from the International Amateur Athletics Association (now

World Athletics). She accepted the challenge and eventually completed the four levels of World Athletics certifications — always with the same goal: to improve her athletes' performances so that they could qualify to represent Kenya internationally. And she continued to work for the KPT, a necessity since her coaching was, and remains, unpaid.

The transition was straightforward. Most of the athletes she coached already had a history of relying on her for advice. "I was quick off the block [to step in] when our coach was absent, so it was a natural progression. At first, I didn't think of coaching as my life's work, but gradually it sunk in that coaching was what God made me to do."

Over time, Carolyne became increasingly involved with Paralympic sport and the Deaflympics, encouraged by her coach, the late Herina Malit, then the head coach of Kenya's Paralympic team. "Herina was passionate about helping people living with a disability. I used to join her when she was coaching them, and the way she managed them got to me, and I committed to treating all athletes, whether Deaf, Paralympian, or elite the same." As national coach for the Deaflympics, Carolyne coached her athletes to four gold medals at the 2012 World Deaf Athletics Championships and was named Coach of the Year. She also coached at the 2015 African Games (formerly the All-African Games), the 2016 World Deaf Athletics Championships, the 2018 Commonwealth Games, the 2016 and 2020 Olympic Games, the 2020 Dubai Grand Prix qualifying round, and the 2021 Deaflympics.

Another passion was refugee sport, fostered by Tegla Chepkite Loroupe, the champion distance runner and marathoner who was also Kenya's peace ambassador and founder in 2003 of the Tegla Loroupe Peace Foundation.[25] Like Carolyne, Loroupe was an employee of KPT. The company was a staunch supporter of sports and athletes, allowing time to train and often keeping "stars" such as Loroupe on the payroll even when they were competing abroad.

---

[25] Tegla Loroupe Peace Foundation (website), Tegla Loroupe Peace Foundation, accessed September 20, 2023, https://teglapeace.org/.

In 2015, the United Nations High Commissioner for Refugees (UNHCR) formed a partnership with the Peace Foundation to "identify, mentor, and train talented refugee athletes in Kenya."[26] The foundation helped in the selection and training of twenty-nine female and male athletes from South Sudan, Somalia, Ethiopia, and the Democratic Republic of Congo. Trials for the IOC's Athlete Refugee Team before the 2016 Olympic Games led to the selection of five of the African athletes to the team, a historical first. Carolyne, who was one of the coaches, said it was a unique situation. "After training, they would talk about how they fled their country, mostly on foot, and how they had to sleep in caves before reaching the Kenyan border. At least they now had a place to call home and they also became part of my family in Kakuma, a town in Northern Kenya that is the site of a UNHCR refugee camp and where I lived while I was coaching them." Although COVID-19 ended Carolyne's coaching of the refugees, they forged a strong bond and remain connected.

The WCIP Effect

Carolyne learned about the WCIP from Paralympic coach Joan Nagujja, her Ugandan counterpart. Missing the first application deadline due to communication challenges with NOCK, she persisted and rallied support from Athletics Kenya, an essential step in the application process. The next hurdle was acquiring her airplane ticket from NOCK, which once again proved to be difficult. Discouraged, she contacted Francis Paul, who had first encouraged Carolyne to try heptathlon and was now NOCK secretary-general. "He gave me the number of the agent who was issuing tickets; I called him and arranged to meet him at the NOCK office to retrieve my tickets, and that's how I came to Gold Coast."

The WCIP proved inspirational for Carolyne. "It was a beautiful moment when the women from the Commonwealth family

---

[26] "IOC Refugee Olympic Team Rio 2016," International Olympic Committee, accessed September 20, 2023, https://olympics.com/ioc/refugee-olympic-team-rio-2016.

converged together for a common cause: sharing their journeys as women in coaching. It helped us to understand that as women coaches we face the same challenge, which is being looked at as a woman and not recognised for our brains and abilities [to coach]. It was a chance to interact and build networks."

Carolyne Kola in Kakuma with athletes from the Refugee Team

COVID-19 Posed Challenges

In her coaching, Carolyne does not differentiate between athletes with a disability and those without. "I don't look at their physical disabilities, but at what they can do. My goal is to open a training camp for all to train and prosper in their areas of choice. Some of our athletes come from very poor backgrounds and you sympathise with them; you have to chip in and help them. If I had a training camp, they could simply come to it and live and train. So many of our athletes could do much better in such a facility; they languish because, in Kenya, the focus is mostly on the able-bodied runners. I never look at disabilities as a hindrance."

Equipment challenges have always dogged Caroylne's efforts. For example, in preparing for the Tokyo Olympics, she tried and failed to get modern vaulting fibres for her combined event athletes despite campaigning hard for her well-wishers to chip in. Even more troublesome was COVID-19's impact on training, most of which had to be conducted virtually. "As a coach, you need to be present to correct, explain, and demonstrate so the athlete grasps the technique."

The first case of COVID in Kenya was reported on March 13, 2020. Up to and including December 2022, the country endured at least five waves of the pandemic. Over that time, prophylactic measures included school closures, banning of social gatherings, halting all movement in and out of Nairobi, and national dawn-to-dusk curfews. All restrictions were lifted on March 11, 2022.

However, while somewhat effective in curbing the pandemic, according to the Conversation, "The COVID-19 pandemic has made matters worse for the over two million people living in Nairobi's informal settlements — about 56% of the capital's population. Because families are not growing their own food in such urban areas, paid work is crucial to ensuring they purchase enough to eat. Unfortunately, over a million Kenyans lost their jobs and livelihoods under measures imposed by the government to curb the spread of the corona virus. These measures included lockdowns, curfews, business closures, and travel restrictions."[27]

Carolyne recalled the period leading up to the Tokyo Olympics (July 23 to August 8, 2021): "There were so many restrictions. For example, before going to Tunisia for a qualifying round for the Paralympics, we had to do a COVID test, and once we got to the camp, we couldn't leave until departure day, and nobody was allowed in. It was so hectic! Able-bodied athletes could qualify for Tokyo in Nairobi, but for Paralympians, we had to compete at three meets

---

[27] Matthew Shupler and Dan Pope, "Kenya's COVID-19 Lockdown Is Forcing People to Make Difficult Food and Household Energy Decisions," The Conversation, April 19, 2021, https://theconversation.com/kenyas-covid-19-lockdown-is-forcing-people-to-make-difficult-food-and-household-energy-decisions-158449.

sanctioned by the International Paralympic Committee: Dubai, Tunisia, and Paris." Her athletes did well in Dubai, winning six gold and seven silver medals. In Tunisia, the totals were four gold, five silver, and three bronze medals. Tokyo was a disappointment as the team only managed a bronze medal.

Overcoming Loss and Carrying On

Sadly, Carolyne's husband, Ezekial, passed away on December 6, 1997. She continues to live in Nairobi in her own home, purchased while working with the KPT. Nearby are her three sons and two grandchildren, Carol Mor and Fidal Pascal. After university, Noel joined the Kenya Police Service, Maxwell started his own filmmaking and photography business in Nairobi, and John followed Carolyne into sports and joined the KPT before moving to Doha to work with Qatar Airways.

Carolyne remains as focused as ever on coaching. "I just want to keep on helping the athletes with whom I am working; I will knock on any door to help them. Yes! I am stubborn!"

Chapter Eleven
Jill Perry
Canada

Jill Perry may be short (she's 157 cm, or barely five two) but her trailblazing accomplishments far outweigh her size. She is a chartered professional coach (ChPC)[28] and became a national boxing champion in her thirties. She owns and operates a legendary boxing club, is a sought-after boxing coach, "gives back" as a dedicated mentor to the next generation of women boxing coaches and is an exemplar of living with cancer.

Jill was born in Transcona, an east-end suburb of Winnipeg, Manitoba, on November 5, 1966, to Don, an electrician with the Canadian National Railway, and Muriel, a stay-at-home mom. The city is in the heart of Central Canada and is equidistant from the Atlantic and Pacific Oceans. Its name originates from the Western Cree word *winipīhk*, which means "muddy water," and it is homeland of the Métis

---

[28] "About the ChPC and Registered Coach Program," Coaching Association of Canada, accessed September 20, 2023, https://coach.ca/about-chpc-and-registered-coach-program.

Nation and traditional territory of the Anishinabe (Ojibway), Ininew (Cree), Oji-Cree, Dene, and Dakota; centuries before European arrival, it was a trading centre for Indigenous Peoples.

The Perrys were a working-class family. "We lived a quiet life. My mom made sure that the three children — Janine, Robert, and me — were active in sports. She coached Janine's hockey team when hockey was a new sport for women and she walked me to swimming lessons in the winter, and as I recall, it was a long, cold walk! Swimming was a necessity because we spent much of the summer at Brereton Lake, in the Whiteshell Provincial Park." Like many Canadian girls, Jill was also a Brownie, the branch of the Girl Guides of Canada for seven- and eight-year-olds (now renamed Embers in an effort to become more inclusive), which she found less than enjoyable because she never quite fit in.

Left to right: Bah Chui Mei, Lini Kazim, Mpho Madi, Jill Perry and Martine Dugrenier at the WCIP closing reception.
Photographer: Murray Rix, Rix Ryan Photography Qld. Supplied by Griffith Uni Gold Coast, Queensland.

Finding Her Own Way

Having siblings who were older and bigger than her — Janine is six years older, and Robert is three years older — drove Jill to find ways to make her presence felt. Janine, who excelled at all sports, was considered the athletic star of the family. Tired of comparing herself negatively to her physically stronger sister, Jill began to venture into sports other than those favoured by Janine, although she did try traditional sports such as soccer and baseball, but notes, "I was so short, people couldn't pitch to me." And of ringette, Jill says, "My sister was a superstar, and I was just okay; I lived very much in her shadow. And team sports just didn't come to me."

Jill describes herself as a hard worker, a "grinder" at the sports she played as a youth. She turned her short stature to her advantage, becoming tough and resilient. She also credits her parents with raising her to be "highly independent and resourceful, which has benefitted [her] throughout [her] life."

By her teens, Jill preferred working and making money to sports. "I worked at the Westin Hotel in the banquet department as a server. I saved most of my money, but did indulge in a few things, like a new car when I was just sixteen. I wanted lots from life and, if I wanted something, I had to work for it."

Jill attended Kildonan East Collegiate, a technical secondary school; a favourite subject was graphic design. Her first job upon graduation was with the advertising department of Loblaws, a Canadian supermarket chain with stores in the provinces of Alberta, British Columbia, Manitoba, Ontario, Québec, and Saskatchewan. Finding herself with spare time, she decided to pursue recreational sport. Her choice was bodybuilding, and before long, she was competing — to the consternation of her father, who once said, after she purchased new gym clothes, "Why don't you buy a dress and go on a date?"

But for Jill, bodybuilding was a game-changer, as she discovered the sheer pleasure of doing well at a sport. Never one for half measures, she added running and half marathons, aerobics, and fitness classes. Then, at the age of twenty-eight, she discovered boxing. "As soon as I tried it, I loved it. I loved that it was aggressive and yet you have to be smart about it. It's challenging and it's scary and it's different; I liked that. Given the sizes of my sister and brother, I always had to be scrappy, and boxing suited my personality. I was also extremely independent, and boxing was totally me."

After five years in the workforce, Jill realised that it was time to switch directions and decided that meant earning a university degree, but not in Winnipeg, even though she was well established there. She broke up with her long-term boyfriend, got rid of her apartment, sold all her possessions, and in 1991, moved to Ottawa to study commerce at Carleton University, with a view to go into marketing. "Fresh start!"

After graduation in 1995, Jill worked for a year before joining Corel, a professional graphic design software firm, as a product specialist. During her four years with the company, she travelled the world. Jill was laid off when the tech bubble burst in 2001 and many companies, including Corel, came crashing down, so she decided to take a year off, exhausted from all the travel. It was time, she felt, to invest in herself. It was a wise decision that set her boxing career on fire. "I had a severance package and vacation time I had never taken and decided to steal a year of my retirement. I trained like a madwoman and got so fit, and my boxing grew exponentially."

The week before the year was up, Jill applied for three jobs, got an offer, and spent the next twelve years with Semiconductor Insights, a technology consulting company where she was responsible for marketing.

Throughout this time, Jill's her love affair with the boxing world continued, centred around the Beaver Boxing Club, which she had joined in 1998 at the age of thirty-two, and its legendary coach, Joey Sandulo.

Her move to Ottawa may have been a fresh start, but for a boxer, it was a late start. Not only was Jill older, but there were also few women boxers with whom she could spar and compete. "I should have been done before I started because, at that age, you're already done. No one told me that, so I didn't make it an issue. I was beating girls who could have been my kids and I was so into the sport. I loved the culture, how the sport is played, the intensity." Jill was equally excited about fitness, swimming each morning, and doing triathlons in the summer when boxing went into hiatus (and even placing occasionally through sheer toughness).

Jill fought her first bout as an amateur boxer in 2001 at the age of thirty-four. In 2005, at the age of thirty-nine, she won the national 57-kilogram title, breaking the record for oldest Canadian champion, which still stands. She added a second national title a year later.

Possessed of inherent leadership qualities, she started winding down her boxing. "I retired at forty, having done all I could, so there were no new challenges." Jill gradually began helping Sandulo, with whom she had developed a close friendship. "He was my coach and then we were colleagues, and as he grew older, I started helping him with the other boxers, developed a registration system for the club, booked travel, handled all the driving. Coaching seemed to come naturally to me. Also, the stars aligned that I had an older coach and was ready to help him. I was mentored by him for a long time without realising I was being mentored. And I wonder if I would have coached had he been in his fifties; he would have been more in charge and may not have needed my help."

Forced Retirement

By 2011, Sandulo was fully retired and had entrusted the club to Jill, who became the not-for-profit club's president and head coach. Concurrently, she retired from Semiconductor Insights when she was diagnosed with cancer. As difficult as it was to receive the news, she is convinced that her evolution into a remarkable coach could not have happened had she still been working in technology. "In some ways, cancer was a gift because it allowed me to spend time doing what I love — boxing and coaching. That is my positive takeaway from my cancer."

Over three weeks, Jill had gone from being healthy to having appendicitis to being a cancer patient. It started with the appendectomy. Since there was no sign of the appendix being cancerous, the surgeon decided to remove it laparoscopically, a procedure that spread the cancer throughout her body. "I went from being surgically treatable to having stage IV cancer. The doctor felt badly, but I bear her no ill will; it was an honest mistake. And again, it has allowed me to do the things I love, so I take that from it."

Jill's ordeal continued several months later when she travelled to Montréal to undergo surgery with a specialist in intraperitoneal chemotherapy, a type of chemotherapy infusion that treats some cancers of the abdominal region. Although hers was considered to be a very aggressive cancer, the surgeon decided to take a chance on Jill because her fitness and mental toughness convinced him that she could tolerate the invasive procedure.

In Jill's words: "They cut you open, eviscerate you, and cut out all the cancer bits. Then you are filled with a hot chemotherapy fluid for ninety minutes and you are rotated on the operating table to allow the fluid to work its way through the abdominal cavity. Mine was a thirteen-hour procedure. I was in the ICU for five days and in hospital for six weeks, during which time I almost died from sepsis and lost twenty-six pounds.

"I'm stage IV and am never going to be cured. They call me 'unremarkable,' which in medical terms means 'awesome.' In other words, it means the cancer is inactive; there's something there, but it's not doing anything."

Throughout her ordeal, Jill's husband, Jim English, was by her side. The two, who recently celebrated their eighth wedding anniversary, met while swimming with a master's group at Carleton University. Jill usually swam in the morning but, for reasons she no longer recalls, she chose to attend an evening session. The two were swimming in the same lane when Jill touched Jim's heel, a signal swimmers use when wanting to pass someone. "It's rude to touch someone's feet unless you want to pass; I didn't really want to pass but wasn't paying attention so that started us talking."

At the time of Jill's diagnosis, they had been living together for four years. Jim thought her boxing passion was "very interesting," and he became her biggest fan. He stayed with her throughout her hospitalisation in Montréal. Family members and friends from the boxing community also provided support. Jill was away from the club for six months, although it took another six months to feel well enough to return to full-time coaching. In the interim, Jim and the club members ensured that things ran smoothly.

Acquiring Coaching Credentials

Again and again, Jill credited Joey Sandulo, who died in December 2019 at the age of eighty-eight, as being essential to her progress as a coach. He was widely respected as a boxer, coach, official, and administrator, and is credited with the development of numerous Canadian champions, including Jill. His support enhanced Jill's credibility, and many of his relationships became hers. "I very much benefitted from my association with him as a powerful and recognised coach. Otherwise, I would not be where I am today. Only one coach gives me a hard time about being a woman, and my club is bigger and more successful than his and I and my athletes are more successful than his."

Early on, Jill recognised the importance of coach education as she set out to be the best possible coach. In 2004, Peter Wylie, a "female-positive" male coach, arranged for her to enter the Coaching Association of Canada's National Coaching Certification Program that enabled women boxing coaching to enrol in Levels 1, 2, and 3 Technical. She also completed the practical element and felt well prepared to coach — until she decided to take a virtual master's degree in high performance coaching at the University of British Columbia (UBC). "That's when I realised I knew nothing; it was amazing."

Jill credited the course with exposing her to many different sports, which was critically important for her. "The first year was a huge game-changer; it got me out of the silo of my sport, and I felt like such a different coach, so much more informed. If I had stayed within boxing, I wouldn't be the coach I am today."

Another game-changer was the Women Coach Internship Programme, sponsored by the Commonwealth Games Federation in conjunction with the 2018 Commonwealth Games in Gold Coast, Australia. Jill was being mentored by Shelley Coolidge, ChPC, an ice hockey coach she met through the UBC programme who suggested that she apply for the WCIP. Up until her acceptance, Jill had been given only one coaching assignment by Boxing Canada. Now she had the chance to learn, grow, and show her potential to her sport's leaders. "The WCIP was my springboard to next-level-coaching. I had all this coach education but lacked practical experience. Now I got to coach at the national championships, a lead-up to the Games, was able to contribute during the Games because of my education, and was part of the team of head coach (who had five Olympic Games to his credit), technical director, sport psychologist, and athletic trainers. I got to show them that I am a great team player ... As a woman coach, I thought differently and brought different ideas to the table, and they saw that the athletes benefitted.

"I loved the WCIP, the structure, getting up and spending the first part of the day with nineteen other interns. It got me excited and gave me a special purpose and energy ... I am really big into hearing what coaches from other sports are doing because there's always transferable skills and information. It is so important to get out of our silos, and the WCIP provided that. And the energy has been maintained; these coaches are my network; all are respected within their own sports, and we've all been through this experience. I value and seek out their opinions."

COVID-19 Demanded Adjustments

Jill's experience with the pandemic revolved around being a club owner striving to survive provincially mandated lockdowns. From March 2020 until June 2021, the Province of Ontario's approach seesawed through three states of emergency: March 17 to July 24, 2020; January 12 to February 9, 2021; and April 7 to June 2, 2021. It wasn't until April 27, 2022, that all remaining measures, directives, and orders ended. As challenging as the pandemic was, Jill managed several positive outcomes, including launching a virtual boxing club with Jennifer Huggens, a woman coach and club owner. "Teaching virtually was new to me and, in many ways, it helped me to further develop my coaching skills."

Virtually and through socially distanced training, Jill worked with Emelia Dermott, a national team member and a designated Next-Generation Athlete,[29] giving her access to a federal government funding programme for future Olympians and Paralympians. "In some ways, COVID was a gift to Emelia. In 2018, she came from Toronto to Ottawa to work with me and transform into a senior athlete. We identified skill gaps and worked like mad in skills. She was able to really focus and now is a different boxer, open to learning and improving."

Then, when COVID broke out, Emelia returned home to Toronto, and Jill had to figure out how they could work remotely. It was another learning experience for her. "COVID forced me to develop as a coach; I had to leverage my coach education and experience to keep Emelia moving forwards and motivated. Training came with challenges, and being in two different cities was just one of them. Workout plans were written and shared, and before each workout, we discussed the plan, and I provided a list of follow-up questions for us to discuss afterwards. The quality of work remained high and much of that can be attributed to the high degree of communication we put into the programme. My communication skills as a coach grew and my thought processes changed."

Once restrictions were lifted, Jill focused on rebuilding her club to prepandemic levels of business, and her youth team is now bigger than ever. "During the pandemic, I wrote a grant application, which was awarded. I put the funds towards developing new programmes and expanding others. I was able to invest in my coaches and provide them

---

[29] Jessica Barrett, "Next Gen Initiative to Power Aspiring Olympians for Future Success," Canadian Olympic Foundation, July 21, 2017, https://olympic.ca/2017/07/21/next-gen-initiative-to-power-aspiring-olympians-for-future-success/.

with access to training. None of that would have happened without the grant, and so, when we were able to reopen, we were ready."

Planning the Future

When the time comes for Jill's retirement, she will turn management over to the replacement she has already picked out. She is mentoring him and letting him make decisions as she reinvents the club with his input. Her health will always be a question mark, so it is important to have things in place "just in case." For now, she remains the club's president and head coach but plans to split her duties between two coaches, one who is administratively strong and a second who will become head coach. "The club has a long history and a culture that remains the same as it was when I first walked in the door. It once received free rent from the City of Ottawa, but that is no longer possible. Paying rent was an adjustment at first, but we did it. In fact, we are still able to offer inexpensive memberships and, for kids and families in need, we provide free access to sport. Serving our community and providing affordable sports programming is what drives us, that and training champion boxers. The club is now bigger than it has ever been, and I am always mindful of the obligations I'm creating for the next president and head coach."

Jill explained that the job is now too big for one person, which is why she is intent on splitting the duties, with one person focusing on the business and the other on boxing. Each job requires a specific skill set, and both are vital to the continued success of the club.

The club is large, with 260 members; the ten coaches, Jill included, are all volunteers. "We volunteer because we love the sport. Each coach commits to certain nights or programmes, and we just make it work."

She has one employee. As the "amazing" business manager, Ghous Bilal has played a vital role in the club's growth. Along with the aspiring national team members, there is a strong recreational base. Memberships are given to youngsters who cannot afford the fees, the coaches are paid to complete the National Coaching

Certification Program (NCCP),[30] youth athletes are encouraged to volunteer with the younger classes, and athlete travel is paid by the club. "I've had many great experiences through sport, and I want those I work with to share similar experiences. When they win, I win, and I love winning!"

Davidson Brumarie listens intently to the instructions of his coach, Jill Perry. Photo Credit: Lucas Gordon

Commitment Outside the Ring

Jill enthusiastically shares her expertise with colleagues, provincially and nationally. As the past chair of Boxing Ontario's High Performance Committee, a role she loved and where she felt she could contribute the most, she helped to move the sport forward in her province. "I am not afraid to speak up; I keep things moving, and I like that. I have a really good eye for talent and like to connect people with opportunities and leverage my connections." She is also part of Boxing Canada's coaching pool, serves as a member of its Coaching

---

[30] Offered by the Coaching Association of Canada.

Development Advisory Group, and holds a 1-Star coaching certificate from the International Boxing Association. Colleagues have described her as essential to the creation of Boxing Ontario's Strategic Plan for 2020–2024; one of its formative pillars is development pathways, another of her interests. An outspoken advocate of mentorship, Jill has twice served as a mentor coach for Commonwealth Sport Canada's Women Coach Internship Programme.[31] She is also a strong advocate for gender equity and the advancement of women's boxing.

Her coaching assignments increased and included serving as an assistant coach for Boxing Canada at a training camp held at the US Olympic and Paralympic Training Center in February 2022, where she helped athletes prepare for the Continental Boxing Championships to be held in Guayaquil, Ecuador. She was the team lead at the Eindhoven Box Cup in the Netherlands in June 2022, a coach at the Commonwealth Games in Birmingham, England, in July 2022, and supported boxers at the King of the Ring tournament in Boras, Sweden, in November 2022. Also in November, Jill was elected to a two-year term on Boxing Ontario's board of directors.

Jill is, beyond doubt, an inspirational leader and decision-maker, in the coach's corner and in her sport's boardroom.

---

[31] Sheila Hurtig Robertson, "Commonwealth Women Coach Intern Program (WCIP)," Commonwealth Sport Canada, accessed September 20, 2023, https://commonwealthsport.ca/about-cgc/wcip.html.

Chapter Twelve

Bah Chui Mei

Malaysia

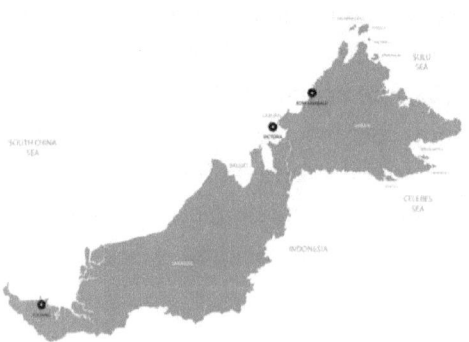

Kuala Lumpur (KL), Malaysia, is home to a soft-spoken lawn bowls coach whose calm demeanour belies her steely determination to bring out the best in her Para bowlers.

For many years, Bah Chui Mei[32] combined her competitive drive — she represented Malaysia at three Commonwealth Games — with her position as senior draughtsperson in the Malaysian Public

---

[32] Bah explains Chinese names: "My surname is Bah and my given is Chui Mei. My dad's surname was Bah and his given name was Bow Kam. According to Chinese tradition, if the father's name is Bah, so the children, both boys and girls, will be given that surname. The boys will pass the surname to their sons and daughters. For example, my nephew's name is Bah Xhan Fhong because my late brother's surname was Bah."

Works Department (PWD), the federal government department responsible for construction and infrastructure maintenance. Creating confidential architectural drawings for the police and armed forces, she worked there from 1980 until her mandatory retirement in 2020. Nowadays, she supports the Malaysian Blind Sports Association (MBSA) as a part-time administration executive while coaching her country's top Para bowlers at major international events.

Bah was born in KL on August 7, 1960, to Bah Bow Kam, a policeman who died in 2014 at the age of seventy-eight, and Lee Jee Foong, who lives with Bah. Bah is the eldest child. Her adoptive sister, Bah Chui Phing, is of Indian Punjabi origin. Her sister Bah Chui Fong was diagnosed with acute leukaemia and died in 1979 at the age of sixteen. In 2009, her brother, Bah Cheng Yein, was killed in a traffic accident at the age of forty-two, leaving his wife, Ivy Chong Wan See; son, Bah Xhan Fhong; and daughter, Bah Suun Faye.

Bah's early years where characterised by moving from place to place as Bah Bow Kam wasn't stationed permanently in any location. When she was an infant, the family moved to Singapore where they lived until 1963, when her father decided to return to KL. It was a pivotal time in the history of Malaysia, which lies along the Strait of Malacca and historically has experienced much turbulence.

British involvement in Malaya, as the region was then known, began in 1786 when the East India Company established a trading post on Penang Island. In 1896, a federation of small Malay states — Pahang, Perak, Selangor, and Negri Sembilan — became the Federated Malay States with KL as its capital. Malaya and Singapore were captured by Japan during World War II and remained occupied until September 1945. The Federation of Malaya was created under British protection in 1948; independence was achieved in 1957. The federation was renamed Malaysia in 1963, and included Singapore, thirteen Malay states, three federal territories, and Sarawak and Sabah, which are on the island of Borneo. In 1965, Singapore became an independent nation. Chinese Malaysians, such as Bah and her family, are Malaysian citizens of Han Chinese ethnicity and form the country's second largest ethnic group after the Malay majority.

In 1967, Bah's family left KL for Butterworth, a large urban town near George Town, the capital of Penang, a state located on Malaysia's northwest coast. It was here that Bah started school, enrolling in St. Holy Infant Jesus Primary School. Two years later, they relocated once again, this time to Alor Setar, the capital of Kedah State where they remained until Bah Bow Kam retired in 1990.

Bah studied at the St. Nicholas Convent, a girls-only school, until the age of fifteen. Bah Bow Kam's final transfer took them to Bukit Mertajam, the administrative centre of the city of Seberang Perai in Penang. There, seventeen-year-old Bah completed her formal education at St. Marguerite Convent School, earning a certificate in education. Convent schools were a legacy of the British colonial period when Christian missionaries established institutions that provided primary and secondary education in English. Most were single gender and fee-paying.

Bah, whose mother has described her as a mischievous, fun-loving, and determined youngster, remembers her childhood as a time of constant activity even as she followed an established routine. She and her siblings enjoyed travelling back and forth to school in a trishaw (a light three-wheeled vehicle with pedals). After school, she helped her mother with household chores and then settled down for an afternoon nap. Evenings were spent at the local playground followed by studying and doing homework for an hour and a half. Bedtime was 9:00 p.m.

Structure has stayed with Bah throughout her life. "I realise now that both my work and my coaching are driven by routine. When asked to describe my childhood, it is amazing and incredible to see how routine is the reality of my life ... My parents brought me up to be a responsible person."

When Bah graduated from secondary school in 1977, she hoped to attend university, but the fees were beyond her family's means. "I told my mother to give the funds to Bah Cheng Yein because, in a Chinese family, the boy comes first." She was satisfied to have her job with the PWD, which supported her sporting interests by approving leaves of absence when required and providing training allowances. "I had everything I needed."

Bah Chui Mei

Journeying to the International Stage

From a young age, all aspects of athletics appealed to Bah. However, by the age of fifteen, she decided to specialise in javelin. Partial to throwing, she was also attracted by the high level of fitness and agility the discipline demands. Lacking speed, she relied on her coach, the late Martin Ham, for innovative exercises to develop her running ability. After leaving school, she continued training with her coach and competed as a state athlete and at the federal level with the

Malaysia Amateur Athletic Union (now the Malaysian Athletics Federation). Her hopes of competing with the national team dimmed when she failed to meet the standard required by the Olympic Council of Malaysia (OCM). When not throwing javelin, Bah played interdepartmental volleyball and table tennis for the PWD's sport section and at the interstate level. "Sport gives you a positive mindset and makes you a better person in all aspects of life; you feel strong and healthy."

In 1987, at the age of twenty-seven, Bah decided to stop training for javelin because of the demands of daily workouts and because she felt beyond the age to produce optimal results. When she found the transition difficult, she looked around for a sport she could pursue in her later years, not necessarily focusing on competition but for exercise and to stay fit; lawn bowls fit the bill. "It takes a lot of mental skill, accuracy, and consistency. I found it interesting, and I was good at it." Her choice would later prove to be fortuitous. Selected in 1991 by the Commonwealth Games Federation, Malaysia was to host the 1998 Commonwealth Games, lawn bowls was on the sport calendar, and Malaysian players were badly needed. Why not? Bah thought. I'll try out for the fun of it even though the sport has no history in Malaysia.

By 1995, Bah had become one of a group of twenty potential international-level bowlers trained by Peter Belliss of New Zealand, then one of the world's best. By 1998, the group had been pared to seven bowlers who had been given a strong foundation by Belliss and Australian coaches Robbie Dobbins and Lachlan Tighe, all of whom innovated strong and practical training programmes.

While the bowlers prepared for the Games, the National Sports Council of Malaysia (NSCM) provided food and lodging, training facilities at the National Sport Complex (located in the affluent KL suburb of Bukit Jalil), transportation to venues, and generous financial allowances that increased as medals were won at various important competitions. "The only thing was, we had to train every day!" Bah's department granted her approval to train as required and continued to pay her salary. In return, she was obliged to keep up to date on her work commitments, ensuring very full days.

Bah was trained for the Fours but, one month before the Commonwealth Games opened, she was suddenly told that she would be skipping the Pairs. Although told that she should consider the change a promotion, she was unhappy and had difficulty adjusting to a role for which she was not trained. She and her teammates won five and lost five games to end up in fifth spot in their group. Ironically, the Fours won the bronze medal!

Future competitions produced better results. Between 1999 and 2007, Bah won three gold medals at Southeast Asian Games; two bronze medals at the 2001 Asia Pacific Bowls Championships; and made appearances at two more Commonwealth Games, including Manchester in 2002, where she played the lead on the Fours. Being up against England in a live-televised quarterfinal game was "horrible," and she recalled, "Afterwards, I told my mental trainer that I wanted to block everything. Still, I learned the importance of being very strong mentally, and now I stress this to my athletes."

Transitioning Into Coaching

After the 2006 Commonwealth Games in Melbourne, Australia, Bah's contract as a player ended and the Malaysia Lawn Bowls Federation (MLBF) decided she should build on her lengthy experience and transfer her considerable skills to coaching. Mentored by the former head national coach, Ariffin Ghani, and the former assistant national coach, Choo Yih Hwa, Bah quickly showed that she had potential. She began attending coaching and sport science courses and, before long, was a state junior coach, which eventually led to involvement with the junior and senior national squads.

Assigned to the 2010 Malaysian Games in her first head coach position, Bah led her squad of youngsters to a gold medal. More coaching assignments followed as she began to take coaching seriously. In 2013, Choo Yih Hwa recommended that Bah travel to Hong Kong as her assistant coach of local able-bodied players for a two-week training programme. It was a make-or-break experience. "The Hong Kong players are very challenging, and I wanted to see how far I could go with them. They ask a lot of questions, and you have to be able to answer, or else. In the end, they respected me, and that gave me confidence."

Shortly thereafter, Ahmad Rashidi, the president of the Malaysian Bowls for the Disabled Association, asked Ariffin Ghani to recommend a coach for the Para bowlers. Ghani chose Bah, saying she had the capability to understand players. Undertaking special training to prepare for the role, Bah turned to British coach Raymond Smith for advice and tips and added Levels 1 through 3 in both coaching and sport science to become a fully qualified Class A coach.

At the time, the 2014 Commonwealth Games in Glasgow, which had a Para component, were approaching and would be followed later in the year by the 2014 Asian Para Games in Incheon, South Korea. Glasgow was a disappointment because Bah's preferred players were not selected, and so she sat out the Games. Incheon was different. Learning from the Glasgow experience, the MLBF heeded Bah when she insisted that every one of the Para bowlers had to be involved in her training programme. "All were so committed to their training, and I was so happy when the NSCM and the Paralympic Council Malaysia listened when I explained how important it was for the whole team to share the training camp experience." Coached by Bah, the team brought home two gold, one silver, and five bronze medals from Incheon — "a highly satisfactory result." To her surprise, victorious Malaysian coaches are eligible for an incentive programme created by the NSCM, and the Incheon results netted her and her assistants a welcome payday.

WCIP Unsettling, Exhilarating

In 2017, Bah was a part-time national coach for the able-bodied bowlers preparing to compete at the Southeast Asian Games. Then came news that the Commonwealth Games Federation was launching an application process for the Women Coach Internship Programme to take place at the 2018 Commonwealth Games in Gold Coast, Australia. Haslah Hassan, Bah's teammate in 1998 and coach of the national women's team since 2009, notified her of the opportunity. Bah quickly submitted her application to the OCM. She credited the support of Secretary-General Datuk Low Beng Choo with helping her to complete the application form. Her acceptance was confirmed in December 2017. "I was honoured to be selected as it gave me a chance learn to do what I have dreamt of, which is to initiate a proper programme for women in coaching."

Although the WCIP itself was an "overwhelmingly positive" experience for Bah, certain behaviours left much to be desired. A key principle of the programme was on-the-field experience, by which the intern coach was meant to be an integral part of her sport's coaching team. Bah, however, was treated as an observer by Simon Botha, a South African who was the head coach of the Malaysian national squad. "He felt that I was a distraction and was uncomfortable with me, even afraid of me. I wondered why; maybe it was because I am a woman. On the other hand, I took many notes during the competition, and he wanted those notes, so I wrote them into a booklet, complete with a title, a table of contents, and a glossary, which the OCM published!

"I had asked lots of questions because I wanted to learn. In the end, I just followed one of the other male coaches; there was no discussion. I learned that being a woman coach is not as easy as I had thought. My thinking is different…"

For Bah, the WCIP was a confidence builder. She became more outspoken, going so far as to inform Botha that she had to raise her voice and make her opinions known to get what she wanted and needed from the WCIP experience. "I learned that I had to be very aggressive, to insist upon discussions with the other coaches because it was so important to share knowledge … One thing for sure, the WCIP continues to be a success for me because we maintain the bonds of friendship and share our lives. And I am grateful that the WCIP — Sheilagh and Sheila — still believe in all of us."

Bah retired from the PWD on April 27, 2020 — in Malaysia, retirement is mandatory at the age of sixty — and became a freelance lawn bowls coach. She laughingly recalled that her first and only promotion within the PWD came at the age of fifty-eight: "One step up after so many years. Promotion only happens when a woman leaves, and there were so many of us — at least thirty per cent are women — that it was rare."

COVID-19 Brought Hard Times

The devastation that was COVID-19 hit Malaysia with a vengeance. A nationwide lockdown was imposed in March 2020, and extensive restrictions were imposed. Mass religious, sports, social, and cultural activities were prohibited. Only supermarkets, public markets, and grocery and convenience stores could open. Kindergartens, government, and private schools were closed, as were all public and private higher education institutions and skill training institutes. Only essential services remained open. By May 2020, as the pandemic appeared to ease, the government progressively relaxed restrictions only to restore them for six months when the third wave hit in September 2020. In January 2021, a nationwide state of emergency was declared, and parliament and state legislative assemblies were suspended until August 2021.

A total lockdown from June 1, 2021, was extended indefinitely and affected all social and economic sectors, excluding only those deemed essential.

The economic impact of the pandemic was severe. The country's currency was devalued and its GDP shrank. A four-phase national recovery plan was introduced in June 2021 to help ease the economic fallout. By October 2021, however, high vaccination rates and a decrease in severe cases meant that COVID-19 would now be treated as an endemic disease. By January 2022, several movement restrictions were ended and, by April 2022, over 80 per cent of the population and 97 per cent of adults were fully inoculated.

For Bah, the pandemic was an ordeal marked by chronic uncertainty as Malaysia went from one lockdown to another. And as hard as it was for her, she explained that it was much harder for her Para bowlers. None had permanent jobs during the pandemic. Some became jobless because of the pandemic, and others had to deal with unreasonable bosses. Finding herself with time on her hands, Bah decided to embark on intensive housecleaning, leading to the discovery of a termite infestation that destroyed the books and notes she had collected over the years. "When my nephew, Bah Xhan Fhong, and I left home to throw everything away in the garbage, it was after the eight p.m. curfew. The police stopped us, but when we explained the situation, they let us go."

Bah's employer allowed her to work from home on a PWD desktop, which she agreed to share with Bah Xhan Fhong so he could keep on top of his schoolwork. He used it from morning until midafternoon, and she worked at night. She returned to the office in early May 2020 until her retirement.

With all sports activities suspended throughout most of 2020, Bah's athletes trained at home as best they could. Most players with physical disabilities did simulations, playing lawn bowls games online; the players with blindness simply stayed home. Bah learned how to host online meetings, which she used to train them in simulating bowling actions. "Because of their disability, they kept to themselves with their families and so they were able to stay physically and mentally fit."

By mid-2021, the situation began to improve. Slowly but steadily, nonessential shops and food outlets began to open up and noncontact sports resumed, but 1-metre distancing remained compulsory, as did wearing masks at all times and sanitising. By year's end, local competitions resumed, with national and international competitions on hold for another year. Gradually, Bah started to train her bowlers to compete at the National Lawn Bowls for the Disabled Games in May 2022 and the Para SUKMA Games in November 2022. The bowlers won two medals, the silver in men's singles B1 and the bronze in men's singles B7. "It was an improvement for the players, and I was happy for them."

Bah Chui Mei explains the fine points of lawn bowls to attentive bowlers at the Simply Bowls Institute in Hong Kong.

Getting on with Life

In January 2023, Bah joined the MBSA, charged primarily with attracting sponsorships to support participation of athletes with blindness in international tournaments. She is also the lawn bowls head coach of the visually impaired team and continues to revise training programmes for both beginners and experienced bowlers. In March 2023, she led four bowlers to the Twelfth World Blind Bowls Championships in Gold Coast, Australia, where Mohd Zamrie Hasan won the B1 silver medal. A lack of financial support led the MBSA to drop two players and one guide from the team; it was, said Bah, a challenging moment. She hoped that a postmortem would recommend solutions to avoid such actions in the future.

Next, on the recommendation of former national coach, Choo Yih Hwa, Bah led a six-week programme to train bowlers at Simply Bowls, a 1,429-square-metre lawn bowls training centre in Hong Kong. She applied the same training programme she used for able-bodied and Para bowlers in Malaysia.

Financially secure, Bah owns her home, which she shares with her mother, sister, niece, and nephew. "If you are able to do this, why not? I now have time for things I couldn't do when I was working and remain involved training disabled players on weekends."

Bah intends to devote the next ten years to training potential women coaches in the skills to work with both able-bodied and Para bowlers. "The first step is to build a strong foundation in the basics that will enable the bowlers to play for a long time. I want to pass on what I have learned, especially when it comes to building trust. Players and their coach have to trust each other fully, otherwise the relationship won't work." She is pleased that the number of women coaches is growing, albeit slowly. "It's good because the male coaches are finally beginning to see things in a different light!"

Chapter Thirteen

Isabelle Lindor-André

Mauritius

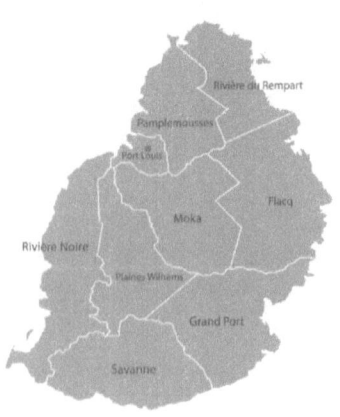

In a society that displays many of the markers of progress — a long tradition of political and social stability, economic and industrial regulatory frameworks, free and fair national elections, low unemployment rates, and rare civil unrest or political violence, the Republic of Mauritius, which lies in the Indian Ocean, is in many ways a beacon for the developing world to emulate.

Overall, Mauritius suggests opportunity and vitality, and Isabelle Lindor-André — athlete, coach, leader, wife, and mother — is a beneficiary of these qualities. She was born on October 24, 1975, to Claude Lindor, an estate agent, and Magalie Lindor, owner of a catering company, in Quatre Bornes, also known as la Ville des Fleurs (City of Flowers), located on the country's central plateau. She has two siblings: Didier Lindor, born in 1978, and Annabelle Lindor, born in 1982, both living in Melbourne, Australia. "I was raised in a loving family, and my parents provided us with every necessity."

The geographically isolated volcanic archipelago that Isabelle calls home was apparently uninhabited until the Dutch East India Company made two attempts — from 1638 to 1658 and 1664 to 1710 — to colonise the place they called Mauritius. The French East India Company occupied the area in 1721 and called it Île de France. Settlement proceeded slowly over the next forty years. In 1767, France took over administration, and slaves were brought in from Africa. Sugar was the main industry, and the colony prospered. During the Napoleonic Wars, the British captured the island and the name reverted to Mauritius. In 1814, the Treaty of Paris confirmed British possession of Mauritius. It became an independent state within the Commonwealth in 1968 and is a parliamentary representative democratic republic.

Today, the Mauritius population of slightly over 1 million is culturally diverse: Franco-Mauritians are the descendants of European settlers; Afro-Mauritians, who may be referred to as Creole, are descended from African slaves; Sino-Mauritians trace their roots to Chinese traders; and Indo-Mauritians' forebears were labourers from India. Regardless of their backgrounds, Mauritians are known for "a nationalised sense of pride ... and unity despite not having a shared language and customs" and are "often considered a global example of successful cultural integration."[33]

This is not to say that Mauritian society is completely progressive. Women, for example, long played subordinate roles as traditional homemakers. They are underrepresented in the National Assembly, holding only 20 per cent of seats, and are paid less than men for equivalent jobs. As with many countries, gender challenges remain,

---

[33] Jeffrey A. Frankel, "Mauritius: African Success Story," Harvard Kennedy School, HKS Faculty Research Working Paper Series RWP10-036, September 2010, https://dash.harvard.edu/bitstream/handle/1/4450110/Frankel_MauritiusAfrican.pdf.

violence against women continues to be a problem, as does physical and sexual harassment.

However, the constitution of Mauritius prohibits discrimination based on gender, and women can pursue employment and have access to government services. And, since education is free up to the tertiary level, girls have access to free primary and secondary education and can also develop professional skills should they wish.

Isabelle Lindor-André

Aiming to Excel

Organised sport was not part of Isabelle's childhood, although unstructured play certainly was. When she was a youngster, Mauritius lacked sports facilities or accessible clubs for small children. However, physical education was part of the secondary school curriculum, providing her with opportunities to experience various sports. So, as a twelve-year-old, she tried athletics, volleyball, and badminton, but it was table tennis that captivated her. Her father and uncles played the game during family holidays and, as a youngster, she enjoyed watching them. In 1987, the sport was formally introduced to her and her classmates by a table tennis coach named Sidney Picon who came to her school — Gaetan Raynal State Secondary School — scouting for potential players. Following his demonstration, several children, including Isabelle, were selected for after-school training. Table tennis being an indoor sport was part of the appeal. "It isn't easy to do sports here because of the heat. I also liked it because it is quick and requires agility and coordination, which I have. This is strange, but I also like the sound of the ball as it hits the table."

"Very excited" at the prospect of training, Isabelle was dismayed when a major cyclone struck and delayed her debut by a week. A common weather event in Mauritius, cyclones typically mean school closures and many days until power, telephone lines, and running water are restored. For those foolhardy enough to venture outside, awaiting them is the sight of blown tin roofs, fallen poles, and broken trees. "This delay was very hard for me because I really wanted to train." Inspired to excel from the beginning, Isabelle aimed be a table tennis champion, and she succeeded, becoming national title holder in her age category in 1996. In 1997, she became senior national champion while still a junior and held the title until 2000. She took a break in 2001 when she gave birth to her daughter, Chloe, returning in 2002 to prepare for the Indian Ocean Island Games, and once again becoming national champion.

Beginning in 1997, Isabelle represented her country at the African Championships, the Francophonie Games, and the Commonwealth Table Tennis Championships. She won gold, silver, and bronze medals at three multisport Indian Ocean Island Games, where the island countries of the Indian Ocean — Mauritius, Seychelles, Comoros, Madagascar, Mayotte, Réunion, and the Maldives — aim to build relationships and improve economic growth.

Building Dual Careers

Also determined to become a teacher, Isabelle earned a diploma in teaching physical education from Mauritius Institute of Education and a bachelor of education with a specialty in physical education from the University of Mauritius. Since 2001, she has taught physical education, mathematics, and English at Lorette Vacoas School. Over the years, she noticed that growing numbers of her pupils had learning difficulties, which she felt unable to address, so in 2017, she completed an online course from the University of Southern Queensland in Australia to earn a master's degree in special education.

In time, coaching overlapped with Isabelle's teaching as she introduced table tennis to youngsters attending her school. In 2016, when the Mauritius Table Tennis Association (MTTA) invited her to take coaching courses, she accepted, always eager to improve her skills. The same year, the MTTA named her coach of the national girls' team, working alongside technical director Cédric Rouleau, who oversees the national teams. She debated accepting the position because, while she was an experienced athlete, her coaching background was minimal. In the end, she signed on because she still retained a high skill level. "I could still play correctly and so believed I could be of some help to the team and of course I had the guidance of the more experienced coaches."

Isabelle held the position for three challenging years, until the conclusion of the 2019 Indian Ocean Island Games, which Mauritius hosted. "As a woman coach, gaining the respect of my counterparts and the athletes was difficult because of tradition — there are few of us in Mauritius — and the MTTA had hired Cédric, a highly experienced professional coach who came from France in 2015. Compared to him, I lacked experience. I did gain the respect of some of the younger players; they were okay, and they listened. Sometimes it was hard for me to motivate and discipline the older players and at times I did not feel very supported."

Another difficulty was finding a balance between her approaches to teaching and to coaching. "My teaching style was not compatible with the coaching style in table tennis at that time; that was frustrating. I kept saying I was too much a teacher to be a coach. Let's say a child isn't working very well in class. I talk to the child, to the family, and go in depth to solve the problem. This approach wasn't expected of me as a coach in Mauritius. The players would come, practise, and leave, which is completely different from teaching, and that was hard for me."

Isabelle also had family responsibilities. She and her husband, Robert André, were married on December 8, 1999. He works in the tourism sector and is currently the manager of a five-star hotel on the north side of the island. They have two children. Chloe is twenty-two and is studying to be a dental technician in Melbourne, Australia, and plans to remain there. Julien is eighteen. After completing secondary school, he will join Chloe in Melbourne for his tertiary studies.

Isabelle stressed the role of her parents, who live next door, in making it possible for her to coach at all. "They really helped me with the children, and that's not unusual. Mauritian parents generally support their children. My mom would look after the children and help with the cooking and housekeeping, and my dad would drive the children to and from school as needed. I am always thankful for my parents' and my family's support."

Isabelle admitted that combining motherhood, teaching, and coaching was "really hard work," but it helped that her coaching career began when the children were older. Chloe pitched in, running the household and helping Julien with his schoolwork. Robert, in step with her parents, was also supportive, driving the children to their various activities when Isabelle and her father were unavailable and handling the grocery shopping.

Australia Beckoned

Nominated by the Mauritius Olympic Committee for the Women Coach Internship Programme, initially Isabelle was intimidated because she didn't know what to expect — she was, after all, far from home and in a small meeting room with twenty-four strangers (the other coaches and the CGF personnel). She remembered that within a couple of hours, everyone had become friends. "It was exciting to meet all the women; it was so natural, although, to be frank, women coaches are rare in Mauritius, so this was an unusual experience." Also, while she had competed at large events, these were her first major Games as a coach. "I think I was more nervous than my players. If I seemed calm, that was just a front."

The men's coach at the time, Patrick Sahajasein, had been assigned to mentor Isabelle during the Games, and she considered his role to be crucial as she assumed responsibility for the three women players. "Even though I was an experienced player, I discovered that coaching is completely different from being an athlete, and having a mentor who shared his knowledge was very important to my development."

Isabelle was struck by the similarities all the interns shared despite coming from eleven sports, twelve countries, and five regions of the world. "Our experiences as women and as coaches were the same, and the bond continues. I stay in touch by reading the messages on the WCIP WhatsApp page."

Aside from her siblings and daughter and her experience at the Games, Isabelle now has another connection to Australia. Visiting Melbourne after Gold Coast, she reconnected with Russell Lavale, a three-time Australian Olympian who is now a coach in Croydon, a suburb of Melbourne. "We met at the 1995 Commonwealth Table Tennis Championships in Singapore, when we were both young players. We became really good friends when I got an Olympic scholarship to Melbourne in 1997. We went our separate ways until the 2018 Games and now we communicate regularly. I can say he became a mentor."

During the Commonwealth Games, Isabelle received word that she had been appointed chairperson of her country's National Commission for Women's Sport (CNSF),[34] established in October 1992 by the Ministry of Youth and Sports (now the Ministry of Youth Empowerment, Sports and Recreation, or MYSESR) to educate young girls and women about the benefits of participating in sports.

---

[34] "Commission Nationale du Sport Féminin," Ministry of Youth Empowerment, Sports & Recreation, accessed September 20, 2023, https://mys.govmu.org/Pages/Sports/Bodies/CNSF/CNSF.aspx.

"Since I have been in office, and despite COVID-19, the numbers of women have been increasing a lot. For example, more than one thousand women participate in swimming and aqua Zumba sessions alone. For thousands of Mauritian women, we provide activities to encourage participation in a friendly atmosphere, ranging from aerobics, yoga, tai chi, swimming, aqua gym — to Zumba, line dancing, badminton, walking clubs, and hiking. My duty is to coordinate all the activities aiming at promoting sports for women, not elite sports, but sports for all." She added that hers is a paid position, which she fulfils after finishing teaching at 2:30 p.m.

Noncommunicable diseases (NCDs) are a prime target of the CNSF; the country's rate of NCDs is very high because of diabetes. "Forty per cent of the population is diabetic or prediabetic, and only twelve per cent are active by the standards of the World Health Organization. That is why the government is putting a lot of effort into getting the population to be active and reducing the NCDs."

Isabelle also serves on the board of directors of the Mauritius Sports Council (MSC), which supports the MYSESR in promoting recreational sports. She is chair of the Association for International Sports for All programme, which promotes sports nationwide through its brand name, Active Mauritius, created to encourage regular engagement in quality sports, physical activity, and physical education.

Stressed by the growing demands of her volunteer activities and holding down her full-time teaching position, Isabelle decided to leave coaching to focus on the CNSF. Her days had become hectic, stretching from six in the morning to nine in the evening, and she concluded that she could reach more people through the CNSF than through coaching. In explaining her choice, she said: "Coaching is more about high performance and competition whereas Sports for All aims to get sedentary people out of their houses, to start being physically active, and to improve their health. The results so far are good, and we expect that, by 2025, we will reach thirty-five per cent in terms of an active population. We reach school children with an after-school physical activity programme; an Ageing Well programme for those twenty-four to sixty-five years old; an elderly fitness programme for those over sixty-five and living in residential homes; a Vulnerable Youth programme for correctional centres; and an Exercise in the Workplace programme."

One interesting aspect of the CNSF is its programme, in partnership with the MSC, to train leaders for its walking club. Each leader is assigned a group to monitor for twenty-four sessions and is expected to motivate their walkers to continue walking after the sessions are complete. Other unique features include organising participation in World Walking Day, celebrated every October, to create awareness of the importance of preserving the environment and participating in physical activities and community building. One component consists of holding a mass Zumba class in which hundreds of women participate. "An important aspect of the CNSF is the swimming sessions. Even though Mauritius is surrounded by luxurious beaches, many Mauritians do not know how to swim, and it is even worse for women, but now, more and more women are joining the swimming sessions; in 2022 alone, twelve hundred were registered."

COVID-19 Forced Adaptation

In March 2020, the COVID-19 pandemic reached Mauritius, and the country was placed under a sanitary curfew for two weeks as of March 19, but this was extended to April 15 and then to June 1, with schools to remain closed until August 1. Only essential services operated, and all supermarkets, shops, and bakeries were closed until April 2. Isabelle confirmed that people were confined to their homes, and grocery shopping was arranged alphabetically and only on specified days. All sports were stopped for three months, but once the number of local cases dropped to zero, the government reopened individual activities. As of June 15, beaches, markets, gyms, parks, community centres, and cinemas became accessible to the public with masks and social distancing remaining compulsory. Reopening of schools was moved up to July 1, and by October 2020, full activities had been resumed. The initial lockdown ended on May 30, with restrictions remaining on certain activities and in public spaces and public gatherings. On January 26, 2021, mass vaccinations began.

Mauritius, less affected than most countries by the pandemic, was the first country in Africa to lift the overall ban on sporting activities. The national table tennis team, for example, resumed training on June 8, 2020, after more than seventy-five days of inactivity. According to Cédric Rouleau, a rotation was organised with each player being required to practise two hours daily. Neither the public nor parents were allowed access to the training hall, and face masks were mandatory as players entered and left the facility. Temperatures were taken, sanitisers were in place, and social distancing was observed. Also back in action were swimming, boxing, and athletics.

In anticipation of the return to "normalcy," the CNSF developed an action plan that has focused on operating in small groups. Its twelve regional subcommittees are responsible for organising activities in their respective regions. For much of the pandemic, it was forbidden to hold activities with more than fifty women, although outdoor activities were allowed. Compulsory measures included masking before and after the activity, recording temperatures, social distancing, and using sanitary gel.

In the meantime, the organisation posted regular updates on its Facebook page, which included links for yoga, aerobics, and Zumba sessions for those wishing to follow physical activities from home. "We reached our audience by organising small regional activities. This model worked very well, and we continue in this direction ... We also have a proximity policy that ensures women are picked up from their homes."

Isabelle (centre) leads an activity of the National Commission for Women's Sport (CNSF) which she chairs.

Rebuilding the CNSF after COVID-19

Although Isabelle is no longer competing or coaching, she credits her sport background with being a key factor in her success with the CNSF. She recognises that having been a high performance player gave her status in the eyes of the growing numbers of CNSF participants. "I hope I am a role model for them, that they, knowing that I was an athlete and still play table tennis recreationally, are happy to have a sportsperson as their chair.

"When the women of the CNSF exercised together, they were especially happy to socialise; they were very close knit. During the lockdown, it was the social aspect that was mostly lacking. But you have to keep your faith and not let yourself get down ... The women showed resilience during the pandemic. For a while after confinement, it was necessary to develop other healthy habits ... It was a question of relearning everything."

The CNSF provides training for its trainers. For example, in 2022, two workshops were held to train women coaches in catchball, a team sport that comes from volleyball, but instead of hitting the ball, it is caught and thrown. It originated in Israel and was intended to be a simpler version of volleyball for women and is now that country's most popular sport for adult women.

A special day-long celebration took place on October 27, 2022, the thirtieth anniversary of CNSF's founding, at the Côte d'Or National Sports Complex. It was the first national event since the pandemic began and drew more than 1,200 women. Many CNSF members attended, and the event attracted much publicity about its activities and opportunities. As well as catchball, Isabelle has expanded the activities menu to include cycling, with a view to attracting more young girls; a plan is in the works to conduct an awareness campaign directed at college-age girls.

"Apart from benefitting the physical health of the participants, mental and psychological well-being should not be neglected. When women meet for physical activities, they make friends, and this contributes greatly to their social development."

Isabelle is honoured to be chair of the CNSF and is grateful to the Government of Mauritius and sports minister Stephan Toussaint for their trust. "While I was an athlete, my county encouraged and supported me. This position is an opportunity to give back. I have met women from all over the island with different backgrounds, and their courage inspires me. Some really struggle to make a living, but they don't give up. In fact, they work harder through the difficult times. Witnessing their courage makes me want to work harder for them."

In early 2023, the CNSF held its first residential camp for its coaches, and Isabelle got the opportunity to listen to the women's stories and to talk with them. "Some have experienced enormous difficulties, like losing a child to the sea, but all say they got the courage to move on thanks to the support of the CNSF women. It is so satisfying the see these women flourish and it gives me much self-satisfaction; I believe in the importance of my job and take it very seriously."

Isabelle's work was inspired by the presentation of Joan Smit, International Netball Federation's regional development manager for Africa, during the WCIP session, which Isabelle described as "life-changing." The interns were visibly moved by Joan's slide demonstration of the Netball Safari initiative: "Begun in 2009, it is a grassroots development project that focuses on providing a quality netball experience to children and teachers This method of training and coaching allows for increased integration at all levels and exposes the potential that netball has and influences socioeconomic development."

"When I listened to Joan, she really helped me. It touched me when she described going to isolated villages where she would prepare a netball field and asked children to look after the babies so the girls could play netball. We are trying to include a similar approach in our programmes, such as having Active Mauritius go to the villages and introduce the children to play; Joan influenced my way of thinking."[35]

---

[35] "Interview with INF's Regional Development Manager for Africa, Joan Smit," *World Netball*, June 22, 2020, https://netball.sport/archives/18568.

Chapter Fourteen

Martine Dugrenier

Canada

It may be a challenge to imagine an athlete, no matter how talented, excelling in sports as diverse as artistic gymnastics and freestyle wrestling. Yet that is exactly what Martine Dugrenier accomplished.

Martine, the "surprise" child of Claire Houle and René Dugrenier, was born on June 12, 1979, in Laval, Québec. She has two siblings: Pascal, her brother and godfather, born in 1971, and her sister, Julie, born in 1972.

Martine was raised in the Saint-François neighbourhood that sits at the extreme east of Île Jésus. Some 30 kilometres from the bustle of Montréal and predominantly agricultural at the time of her birth, Saint-François allowed the youngster to enjoy the outdoors and play every sport imaginable out on the street with her neighbours. She was partial to climbing a tree beside her house, the higher the better, much to the consternation of her mother, who sought to divert her into "safer" interests, such as recreational gymnastics.

Following their parents' divorce when Martine was four years old, the sisters remained with their mother. Three years later, they moved to Saint-Vincent-de-Paul, a district in eastern Laval. The change was difficult for Martine. "I remember being sad to lose my friends and my tree." However, there was a silver lining; the move meant that she was ten minutes away from École Georges-Vanier, a local secondary school that housed an artistic gymnastics facility. Once enrolled, she quickly developed a passion for the competitive aspect of the sport, the travel that came with it, and its people, who became her second family.

École Georges-Vanier is part of Québec's unique Sport-études programme, designed for the high performance athlete who maintains high academic standards. Academically and athletically gifted, Martine entered the programme with a clear objective: work hard and earn an athletic scholarship to an American university. "My studies would be paid for, and I could continue to do gymnastics. There is no university league in Canada, so this was my only option and my dream since I entered secondary school."

Stringent Requirements

"Thousands of Canadian athletes ... compete at the highest level of college athletics in the United States. Thousands of USA athletic scholarships are available to Canadian athletes each year, but to receive an American athletic scholarship, an athlete must first be recruited to play at a United States college ... obtain a student visa through the United States State Department, register with the NCAA [National Collegiate Athletic Association] initial eligibility clearinghouse, and sign up for all of the required American college entry exams."[36]

Everything was going according to plan even though Martine experienced frequent injuries. "I was resilient and persistent. Even wearing a cast, I wanted to train, which drove my mom crazy."

According to the University of Pittsburgh Medical Center, "Gymnastics has one of the highest injury rates among girls' sports ... Gymnasts must be both powerful and graceful. They first learn to perfect a skill and then work on making their bodies look elegant while performing it. Gymnasts use both their arms and legs, putting them at risk for injury to almost any joint in the body ... serious common injuries include wrist fractures, finger and hand injuries, cartilage damage, anterior cruciate ligament (ACL) tears, knee and low back pain, spinal fractures and herniated discs, Achilles tendon strains or tears, ankle sprains [and] shoulder instability."[37]

A week before the 1996 provincial championships, when Martine was in Grade 11 and "at my best," she fractured her tibial plateau[38] and spent six months on crutches before undergoing surgery. The injury put her scholarship dream on hold; competing at either a provincial or national championship was a mandatory component of the application process, and neither was possible.

On the advice of her gymnastics coach, François Daviau, in the fall of 1996, Martine opted to enrol in Vanier College, a public (CÉGEP) college in the Montréal borough of Saint-Laurent. While there, she would recover and improve her English before applying for an American scholarship the following year. Required to take physical education, her only available option was a wrestling class led by Victor Zilberman, Concordia University's wrestling coach, with four Olympic Games and numerous World Championships to his

---

[36] "Can Canadian Student Athletes Apply for Athletic Scholarships at American Colleges?," AthNet, https://www.athleticscholarships.net/canada-athletic-scholarships-america.htm.
[37] "Common Gymnastics Injuries: Treatment and Prevention," UPMC, https://www.upmc.com/services/sports-medicine/for-athletes/gymnastics.
[38] A tibial plateau fracture is a break at the top of the shinbone that involves the knee joint as well.

credit. Possessed of a keen eye for talent, Zilberman quickly spotted a future wrestling champion in Martine and set about trying to convince her to switch sports. She proved to be a hard sell. "Gymnastics was my passion!"

Eventually, Martine agreed to give wrestling a try and, during her first two semesters at Vanier College, she enjoyed the sport enough to

Martine Dugrenier

join Zilberman at the Montréal Wrestling Club located in the Montréal YM-YWHA. Before long, Zilberman sent her to the 1997 provincial championships, where she won a gold medal. Next came the national championships in March 1997. "I won a bronze medal, my first at a national championship. I didn't even know the rules of wrestling. I had been doing gymnastics for about twelve years and, after only twenty weeks, I get a national medal in my new sport!"

A week later, at the provincial gymnastics championships, Martine won silver medals in floor and vault. She also brought home the bronze in vault from the 1998 nationals.

Worried that a wrestling injury could prevent her from competing in gymnastics, Martine stepped away from the sport from May 1997 to January 1999 to focus on her first love. After graduating from Vanier College in 1999, she agreed to Zilberman's suggestion that she enrol in Concordia University's athletic therapy programme and join its wrestling team.

Two months into her first semester, Martine injured both ankles during a gymnastics routine, and the decision to stop that sport was made for her. "I had too many gymnastic injuries, the [American] goal was fading away, and I was getting older ..." Daviau was supportive. "He said that wrestling might be an opportunity for me to grow as an athlete. He saw me win that first national wrestling medal and saw something in me that he had never seen when I was doing gymnastics. He thought I could be a successful wrestler ... I told my mom I was ready to see where wrestling would take me."

Journeying into the Unknown

In 1999, when Martine made her momentous decision, women's wrestling was not an Olympic sport, although Zilberman assured her it was coming.[39] She had dreamt of competing at the Olympics as a gymnast, but "Realistically, I knew it wasn't possible. At the time, you needed to be strong in all four events and not specialise in one or two as you can now." So, rather than pinning all her hopes on becoming an Olympic gymnast, she chose to study full time and wrestle at the Canadian Interuniversity Sport (CIS; now U Sports) Championships. Weighing only 54 kilograms, she added weights to her training

---

[39] Women's wrestling debuted at the 1987 World Championships and at the 2004 Olympic Games in Athens.

programme to meet the physical demands of wrestling. The muscle mass, combined with the explosiveness acquired through her years of gymnastics, paid off in medals. In 1999/2000, her first season with the Concordia Stingers wrestling team, she won bronze in the 54 kg weight class. In her second year, she moved up to 62 kg and placed fifth. By her third year, she was CIS champion, a title she held for the next three years, and in 2004, she was named CIS Women's Outstanding Wrestler of the Year. She was the university's Female Athlete of the Year in 2002, 2003, and 2004.

Martine was also making a name for herself with the national team, although, as a French speaker, a lack of proficiency in English hampered her progress. The English names for the techniques differ from the French, and she was not yet bilingual. She remembered competing at her first World Cup in September 2003 and not understanding national coach Leigh Vierling's instructions. Nevertheless, she contributed to the team's bronze medal.

The trials for the 2004 Olympic Games were held in December 2003. Zilberman wanted Martine to wait until the 2008 Games, by which time she would have gained considerable international experience; she disagreed, believing that the sooner she got the experience the better. At the trials, she lost in the 63 kg final. "I was leading 6–0 when I made a basic mistake and was pinned. The loss motivated me to focus on the 2008 Olympic Games in Beijing, China. I knew I would have a good shot at making that team."

Martine's switch to the 67 kg class made sense given her height. "The 67 kg girls fit more with my style of wrestling. I was tall, 1.66 metres, and the 63 kg girls are often shorter and faster getting the legs and scrambling a bit more. With taller girls, it was easier to attack the leg, which was my speciality."

Martine's international reputation grew. At the 2004 University World Championships in Lodz, Poland, she won the 67 kg gold medal. Next came World Championship silver medals in 2005, 2006, and 2007.

Martine's growing public profile led to a startling consequence. In 2007, Rona, a national home improvement company, was sponsoring one hundred athletes, including Martine, to make public appearances, such as signing autographs at one of its outlets. Following the announcement and a photograph in her local newspaper of such an appearance, she received a phone call from a stranger. "The man was looking for his father and, when he saw my photo, he showed it to his mother, who realised that I had to be his half sister. We look alike, and my last name, the same as my dad's, confirmed it. It was a great experience. We stay in touch and see each other a couple of times a year. He is a mechanic, so he takes care of my car. He is part of the family."

Since 67 kg was a non-Olympic weight class, Martine decided to move down to 63 kg and secured that spot for the 2008 Olympic Games. Losing the bronze medal match, she finished fifth overall.

Martine went to the 2012 Olympic Games in London, England, as an eight-time national champion and three-time world champion. Back to competing in the 63 kg class, she again finished in fifth place. It was the last match of her illustrious career. In 2012 and 2013, despite being hampered by a persistent shoulder injury that rendered her inactive and dealing with two surgeries, her goal remained to return to active competition. However, realising that would be impossible, she retired in May 2015. In 2016, she was inducted into the United World Wrestling Hall of Fame. Three years later, she was accorded the same honour by the YM-YWHA Montréal Jewish Sports Hall of Fame and the Concordia University Sports Hall of Fame.

From World-Class Performances to Educational Excellence

Zilberman was adamant that his athletes maintain academic excellence. In Martine's case, he envisioned her as a physical education teacher at Vanier College. And so it was that, throughout her wrestling career, Martine was laying the groundwork for a future that would immerse her in teaching, coaching, and sport administration. In 2002, she graduated from Concordia with a bachelor of science degree, specialising in athletic therapy. In 2004, she returned to Concordia to complete a graduate diploma in sports administration and also began work on a physical education degree at McGill University, which she completed in 2008. Zilberman also insisted that his wrestlers complete the National Coaching Certification Program and Martine achieved Level 3 in 2005.

Adding Coaching to the Mix

Martine's coaching dated back to her teen years when she worked with beginner gymnasts and ran a gymnastics camp. Her formal history with the Canada Summer Games began in 2005 in Regina, Saskatchewan, when she was named to the coaching staff of Québec's women's team.

In 2009, Martine somewhat reluctantly agreed to accept a part-time job as a physical education teacher at Vanier College while doing her master's degree at Université de Montréal (incomplete) and training for the World Championships. "I told Victor there was no way I could train three times a day, teach, and study, but he said not to worry, because it would only be a couple of classes, just a foot in the door. But a teacher went on maternity leave and there I was carrying a full load only one month before the championships!"

A further complication: Martine's first week of teaching coincided with the 2009 Canada Games in Prince Edward Island. As the only woman wrestling coach in Québec with NCCP Level 3, a mandatory requirement for the Games, she coached the women's team and trained between sessions. "It was crazy ... I was teaching, competing, training, and coaching at the same time! But I still won..."

Martine next coached the women's team at the 2013 Canada Games in Sherbrooke, Québec. By 2017, she was coaching the men's team at secondary school tournaments and, consequently, she was named as their coach for the 2017 Canada Games in Winnipeg, Manitoba. "I had travelled for a year with them and knew they could win a medal, and they did. Their bronze medal was the province's first team medal at the Games. It was an awesome experience. I managed the team, so everyone was ready to wrestle at their best. We had a great win against Alberta to get to the bronze medal match. It was so close."

The WCIP Experience

In October 2017, then national coach Leigh Vierling urged Martine to apply for the WCIP. Her mother had died a few days earlier, and Martine completed the application while preparing for the funeral. "It helped me to cope with her death and was an opportunity to look ahead."

Martine saw the WCIP as an opportunity to be part of these Games, an opportunity she'd been denied as an athlete because of its weight classifications. "I try to benefit from opportunities, and it was a really great experience ... I can't put into words all the benefits the WCIP has had on me as a coach ... to see its impact on [women] coaches from around the world, to learn about their experiences ... to realise that in Canada we are really lucky, that I was in a really good situation compared to other coaches. I remember the sharing; we became like a team, and we still feel connected. Meeting every day made the connection stronger and stronger day after day. I had the opportunity to be the first coach in the corner, and that helped me at later coaching assignments.

"To help athletes achieve their potential and meet their objectives is what I wanted to do after I retired. With everything I experienced, I believed I could have a positive influence on young athletes. That was my goal — and to give back because I received so much from being in the sports world. The person I am today is a result of all my learnings from sport."

Selection to the Gold Coast WCIP confirmed that Martine was on track to achieving her goal, and until COVID-19 struck, coaching success ensued. With her on the coaching staff at the 2018 Junior Pan American Championships, the Canadian men's team won four silver and three bronze medals, and the women's team won three gold, one silver, and two bronze medals. At the 2018 Junior Worlds, Montréal's Aly Barghout won the 125 kg silver medal with Martine coaching from the corner, supported by Tonya Verbeek, then men's and women's national team coach. "It was a great experience to coach a male athlete at the highest international event of his age group. I gave him a very specific strategy for every match, and he wrestled his best and made it to the final."

History was made with that match. It marked the first time two women coached a man in a World Championship final. "I know I made a difference in terms of the strategy. As Aly's coach, Victor prepared him and then made me his coach during the competition. To have Victor trust me was huge."

Other appointments followed in quick succession: the Junior Pan Americans in June 2019; the Junior World Championship in August 2019; and the Pan American Olympic qualifier in March 2020, with Martine as an assistant coach. In 2021, she coached at the Junior Pan American Championship where the men's team won one gold, three silver, and two bronze medals; the women's team accounted for one gold, two silver, and one bronze medal. In 2022, she coached at the Senior Pan American Championships, where Québec wrestlers brought home one gold, two silver, and one bronze medal.

Earlier, in October 2019, Martine had added sport administrator to her credentials, becoming executive director of Fédération de Lutte Olympique du Québec (FLOQ), which she had served as volunteer treasurer. "They needed someone who was a Francophone and who had appropriate credentials, so I decided to take on the role to help the FLOQ, which was struggling at the time."

COVID-19 Meant Stringent Restrictions

In Canada, each province and territory approached the pandemic differently, meaning thirteen variations within the country of close to 39 million people.

On March 14, 2020, Québec declared a public health emergency, which continued until June 1, 2022. On March 15, 2020, the government began enforcing physical distancing measures and closed various recreational facilities and venues, and on March 23, all nonessential businesses were closed. From April 7 to July 2, Montréal cancelled all festivals, public gatherings, and sporting events. On April 10, all cultural and sporting events were cancelled provincewide.

In late summer 2020, a second wave emerged throughout Canada, and that September, restrictions limiting private gatherings were reinstated in Montréal and Québec City as regions approached the orange level of alert. Daily case counts periodically broke provincial records, and the Québec government tightened restrictions further. Québec entered a lockdown on December 25, 2020, and put a curfew in place on January 9, 2021. Cases were down by February 2021, so nonessential businesses and schools were opened. In April, a third wave led to more restrictions, and gyms were again closed. The curfew ended on May 28. A fourth wave in August led to the implementation of vaccine passports (from September 1, 2021, to March 12, 2022), which were required to enter many public indoor spaces. Finally, on May 14, 2022, masks were no longer required to enter most public indoor places.

Throughout the pandemic, Martine relied on online instruction to stay connected with the students in her wrestling class at Vanier College. "I sent them a workout and, in a once-a-week Zoom meeting, I explained it and answered questions. Each sent me a video of their workout, which I found motivated them. We also used a running app to encourage them to improve."

Club wrestlers were under the watchful eyes of Zilberman and his son David, an Olympian and now head coach of the Stingers, while Martine focused on administrative duties with the FLOQ. Late in 2021, Martine renewed her connection with the WCIP, serving as a mentor coach to intern Breanne Graham when Commonwealth Sport Canada secured funding for an online Canadian WCIP. It was an opportunity for Martine to build on the positive experiences of Gold Coast and to enhance her mentorship skills — to Breanne's benefit. Breanne said, "Martine has been an amazing mentor ... she consistently raises questions and makes suggestions for me to try ... and to learn how to continue a wrestling programme during a pandemic."

Martine aspires to coach at the highest levels of her sport.

Post-Pandemic Life

Gradually, the devastating impact of the pandemic began to ease. In 2022, Martine was a popular choice as head coach of Canada's team heading to the Junior Pan American Championships. At the 2022 Canada Games, she was the head coach of Québec's men's and women's teams — winners of two gold, two silver, one bronze, and a fourth-place finish overall for the men. Of note: Martine's WCIP intern coach, Breanne Graham, was on Alberta's coaching staff; her squad finished third. And the FLOQ was recovering from COVID challenges; by 2023, it had the highest number of memberships in its history.

Martine's coaching aptitude attracted international recognition in 2022 when she was selected for the International Olympic Committee's Women in Sport High Performance Pathway programme, a four-year initiative that addresses the underrepresentation of women on Olympic, World Championship, and continental teams. "I'm excited to see where the programme will lead me. The first week was more than I expected; I shared a lot with the coaches and improved my knowledge about my leadership. I came back home excited to apply all I learned there and keep the connections. It is an amazing experience to push my leadership skills to a higher level and learn from my leadership mentor Jane Booth and sport-specific mentor Jessica Medina."

On a personal note, Martine is putting down roots with her partner, Louis Bhérer, an experienced cyclist who, from 2006 to 2008, rode from Saint-Félicien, Québec, to Calbuco Archipelago in the south of Chile. Louis, who holds a doctorate in information technology and works for the Bank of Canada, met Martine in January 2018 at a speed dating event, a first-time experience for both and one she registered for at the last minute.

As Martine moves forward, her unique coaching style is certain to benefit the upcoming generation of wrestlers in Québec and beyond. While she knows that the respect she has earned in part results from her athletic accomplishments, she noted that her coaching methodology and carefully formulated strategies are also significant. "When I am with a team, I make sure the personal coaches continue to coach their own athletes. I share my plan and my strategy with them. We work together to do the best for the athletes. I am not above them; we are equals." It's an approach that is certain to take her a long way towards fulfilling her ambition to coach Canadian wrestlers at an Olympic Games.

Chapter Fifteen
Endurance Ojokolo
Nigeria

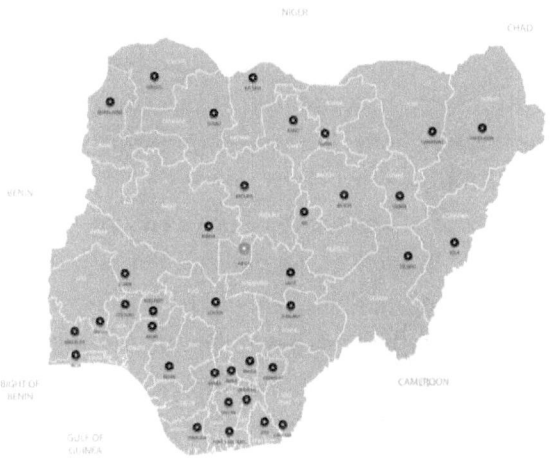

If you search for information about Sapele, a small city on the Benin River in Nigeria's oil-rich Delta State, you'll find mention of eight Notable People. On the list is Endurance Ojokolo, one of Nigeria's all-time great sprinters and notable for her nickname, The Bulldozer, coined to describe her intense, no-holds-barred running style. In a competitive career that spanned sixteen years, from 1992 to 2008, Endurance competed at two World Junior Championships, five World Indoor Championships, six World Championships, one

Commonwealth Games, and one Olympic Games, where she ran in the 4x100 metres final. She won five gold, two silver, and one bronze at five African Championships, and two gold and two silver at three All-Africa Games.

Ten years after her retirement, the athlete turned coach was one of twenty women coaches from around the Commonwealth chosen to participate in the Women Coach Internship Programme inaugurated by the Commonwealth Games Federation at the 2018 Commonwealth Games in Gold Coast, Australia. Her journey from Sapele to the world athletics stage is testimony to her talent, drive, and determination.

Despite minimal facilities, Endurance's hometown of Sapele is known for producing great athletes from boxing, tennis, and football, as well as athletics. Sapele (originally inhabited by the Urhobo people) was colonised by the British during the nineteenth century. Since 1925, it has been a centre for sawmilling and is also known for manufacturing shoes, plastics, and tiles. Local markets provide yams and plantains, cassava, fish, and palm oil and kernels.

Endurance was born in Sapele on September 29, 1975, to Emmanuel Ojokolo, a court clerk, and Rose, who had a stall in the local marketplace. She was the third of seven children: Her brothers are Royal Ojokolo, Evidence Ojokolo, and Reward Ojokolo, and her sisters are Emily Orogan, Benice Efevberha, and Favour Ojokolo.

Endurance noted that hers was a typical African childhood. She explained that, in Nigeria at that time, the female child did most of the chores in adherence to cultural norms that were intended to train her to be a "good wife." From the age of six, she rose as early as 5:00 a.m. to do chores that had to be completed before school started at 8:00 a.m. She fetched water from a distant well, using a rope and bucket, and toted it back home where she poured it into a drum that held 2,000 litres. She then swept the house and the compound. Other chores included washing clothes and dishes. At the time, she was the only female child in the household, Emily having left for England. The child next closest in age to her was Royal, and he was not allowed to do these chores. "When I look back now, I think, Did I really do all that!"

During her years at Sapele's Ugherevie Primary School, from 1982 to 1985, Endurance walked the 3 kilometres there and back despite the incessant heat, marching together with her friends. School buses were unheard-of. Classes ended at 2:00 p.m., and once home, she would take off her school uniform and head to the marketplace to assist her mother, who supported the family by selling provisions such as previously used articles, washing powders, and tissue papers. There, Endurance's duties included placing a tray loaded with items on her head and going into town to sell to the various shops, a distance of 4 to 5 kilometres.

Endurance Ojokolo

Play was a fixture of Endurance's life during her early years, both at school and in the evening after her mother closed her stall at 6:00 p.m. Finishing dinner, she and children from nearby compounds would spend several hours in various activities. Young boys and girls sometimes played together, but that changed as they grew older. A favourite game was kelekele, a form of hide-and-seek played by ten people. "The side of a coin is picked, the coin is tossed, and if the side you picked doesn't show up, you chase people until you catch someone, who then becomes the chaser."

Following Paths Unknown

That Endurance was a talented runner quickly became evident during her primary school days as she competed in the interhouse sports competitions for which Nigeria is known. In Primary 3, she took on students in Primary 6 and inevitably won. This success continued for the next three years, and when she arrived at secondary school as a twelve-year-old, she brought with her a reputation of being able to run fast. "Everybody knew I could run. I wasn't running professionally or going to Sapele Stadium to train; I would just come to races and win."

When she reached Year 7 at Ethiope Primary School in Sapele, the school's games master, Mr. Fred, suggested that Endurance be allowed to run with the seniors so that she could be further challenged. Once again, she was faster than any of them. Knowing only that she loved to run, she took every opportunity to do so, but she wasn't thinking about where it might take her. She knew nothing about the World Junior Championships or the Olympic Games or any other of the world's prestigious sporting events. "They didn't mean anything to me at the time. I just wanted to run, to travel."

One day in 1993, as she competed at the Ethiope Mixed Secondary Invitational Relays, Endurance was approached by the late athletics coach Denis Oboro, who told her that she could run faster if she trained. "Train? I didn't understand what that meant. He told me not to worry but to come to Sapele Stadium the next day at five p.m. But I was thinking that I had to go to the market and help my mom and if I didn't, I would be in trouble." Intrigued, Endurance decided to risk her mother's wrath and, after school, made the 4-kilometre trek to the stadium. "I needed to find out what this training was all about."

Panic was her initial reaction. "There were so many people training, actually training. It was entirely different from running at an invitational meet, too different. This was work, and I wasn't used to it. I was just used to running. So I didn't go the next day or the next or the next ... and after a week, Coach Oboro showed up at my parents' house. He told me I had talent, that I could do better than the people I had seen at the stadium. He was adamant that I would get used to training, so I agreed to give it a go."

St. Ita's Secondary School, which Endurance attended from 1989 to 1993, also played a pivotal role in her blossoming career, with the principal, Mrs. Akpobome, arranging a scholarship so Endurance could combine her studies with competing. This was common practice at the time. "It was a big deal for a school to be the best in sports in Sapele."

Endurance started travelling to race and quickly realised that going to competitions was a pathway to ever-widening horizons, which she craved. Success came quickly as she improved with each outing. First, she was representing her local government. Next came the state junior championships, and before she knew it, she was competing internationally.

Seeking New Horizons

In 1989, at only fourteen years old, Endurance made the courageous decision to leave Sapele for Benin City, 64 kilometres to the north. Sapele lacked a proper training facility; the town's stadium had only a grass track, whereas the stadium in Benin City had a tartan track, and Coach Oboro wanted her to experience that because, he told her, she had the talent to compete on the world stage, including the Olympic Games. "He was a mentor who believed in me."

There was, however, another significant factor in her decision, and that was her mother, who was convinced that, as a sportswoman, Endurance would become too muscular and would be unattractive to men and unable to become pregnant. Rose constantly urged her daughter to stop running, saying, "You can't have children; you need to have your own children."

"That was the mentality where I came from." In 2000, when Endurance became pregnant, Rose was shocked and refused to believe it was possible. "She thought it was a joke until I gave birth to my daughter, Immanuela Aliu.[40] She said: 'Really? Sportswomen actually give birth?' I said, 'Yes!'"

On the other hand, strong support came from her father. She recalled him proudly showing her an article about herself in the local newspaper when she represented Delta State. "Whenever I came home from Benin for the weekend, he gave me lots of encouragement, unlike my mom. He told his wife: 'She's not doing anything wrong; she's just doing her sport, doing something she has a passion for, so leave her be.' We were very close, but after my daughter's birth, I began to get real support from my mom." (Her father, whom Endurance describes as her biggest fan, died in December 1998.)

Endurance's early days in Benin City were far from easy. Initially, she and several teammates "squatted" in a change room within the swimming pool. "It is tough to think about that. How we managed to survive, I really don't know. However, I started understanding what I could actually achieve." By 1990, life began to improve when she competed at the World School Sport Games in Bruges, Belgium. Posting good results entitled her to a monthly allowance from Delta State. Next came the 1992 World Junior Athletics Championships in Seoul, South Korea. Clearly, she was on her way.

Despite the worldwide travels that ensued, Endurance didn't neglect her studies. After secondary school, she studied microeconomics at college. However, thoughts of becoming an economist never materialised; instead, she continued to compete.

During a meet in Birmingham, England, in February 1997, Endurance was contacted by Gianni Demadonna, a former Italian long-distance runner turned agent, who was interested in signing her. She agreed and ran for CUS Milano from 2001 to 2008, when she

---

[40] Dare Esan, "Interview – Born to Run!: Deji Aliu, Ojokolo's Daughter Immanuela Eager to Outshine Parents," Complete Sports, June 4, 2020, https://www.completesports.com/interview-born-to-run-deji-aliu-ojokolos-daughter-immanuela-eager-to-outshine-parents/.

returned to Sapele and retired. A highlight of that period was her appearance at the 2004 Olympic Games in Athens, Greece, where she made the quarterfinals of the 100 metres and finished seventh in the 4x100 metres relay. "It was amazing, a wonderful experience for me. I can't explain it. So many athletes, so many big names. It was totally different from every other competition." Her competitive career ended on a high note at the 2008 African Championships in Addis Ababa, Ethiopia, where she shared the 4x100 metres gold medal with her teammates.

Sprinting great Shelly-Ann Fraser-Pryce of Jamaica (L) and Endurance Ojokolo at the 2019 World Athletics Championships in Doha, Qatar.

Coaching Brings Tribulations and Successes

Endurance did not set out to become a coach after retirement. She considered going into business but, as she said, "My life was track and field; honestly, I couldn't do anything else."

Attending local meets in Sapele, Endurance found herself volunteering to help some of the grassroots sprinters, and gradually her interest in coaching grew. Following three months of coach training, arranged by the Sports Unit of the Nigeria Security and Civil Defence Corps (a semimilitary branch of the federal government that provides protection against attacks and disasters), she began coaching full time with the corps in 2010 and continues to this day. To bolster her credentials, she added training courses offered by the International Amateur Athletic Federation, now World Athletics, and a course on effective coaching at the University of Port Harcourt.

Endurance married Edward Teye in 2011. Their son, also named Edward, was born on November 10, 2013. She continued to coach and placed athletes at youth, junior, and senior competitions. Unfortunately, from the beginning of the marriage, her husband was not supportive, not even when her athletes did well. "He did not understand why I wanted to coach, and that has been very worrying; I got used to it, but trying to manage my career and my husband wasn't easy, even though I tried my best ... it was a shame."

At the same time, Endurance struggled to find acceptance within the ranks of the Nigerian track and field administration. Her successes notwithstanding, officials repeatedly failed to invite her to training camps or select her to coach teams, citing her relative inexperience.

The struggles continued when the time came to apply for the Women Coach Internship Programme to be held during the 2018 Commonwealth Games in Gold Coast, Australia. Upon learning that the same officials were blocking Endurance's application, Chief Tonobok Okowa (president of the Athletics Federation of Nigeria) and technical director Samuel Onikeku spoke out and contradicted the claim of inexperience, noting that she had not only been one of the country's best athletes but had proven her ability as a top sprint coach. Thanks to their intervention, she took her place alongside nineteen other women coaches from around the Commonwealth.

The Games afforded Endurance an important opportunity to showcase her skills. At the pre-Games sprint training camp, her own athletes and those of other coaches showed "massive improvement." "I knew my work would speak for me and that's exactly what happened."

Another supporter was ex-international Olu Sule, now the national athletics coach. He accompanied Endurance to the first WCIP meeting in Gold Coast and served as her mentor throughout the Games. "He is one of the reasons I have never given up on coaching. He has always been there to talk me through situations. He encouraged me to never give up, because that is what 'they' want you to do."

Endurance is philosophical about her struggles. "I let what was said challenge me to become an even better coach, so they had to see the good in me. In Nigeria, most females don't coach and there's no such thing as gender equality. But I never gave up. I kept on coaching my athletes and making sure they were getting better and better, so the officials were forced to recognise me."

In assessing where her life stands today, Endurance noted with pride that "no male coach who has trained an athlete in Nigeria, in poor facilities, has an athlete who has run as fast as mine." The athlete she's referring to is Usheoritse Ese Itsekiri, reigning Nigerian National Sports Festival champion, 2019 African Games bronze medallist in the 100 metres, and 2019 national champion in the 100 and 200 metres. He also competed in sprints and 4 x 100 metres relays at the 2018 Commonwealth Games, the 2019 World Athletics Championships, the 2020 Tokyo Olympics, and the 2022 World Athletics Championships. After he cut his 100 metres personal best from 10:20 to 10:02 at the African Games in Rabat, Endurance was selected to coach at the 2019 World Athletics Championship in Doha, Qatar.

As an athlete, Endurance competed at six World Championships but, she noted, being in Doha as a coach was "strange, not the same at all. As an athlete your only focus is on competing, and as a coach, you have time to note everything that is going on and to learn new things." Although winning an Olympic medal eluded her, her hope now is to train an athlete to accomplish that feat. "I don't care about the colour; I just want an athlete who will fill that space for me, and it could be Usheoritse."

After Doha, other coaching assignments came her way, including the 2019 African Games in Rabat, Morocco, and the 2021 World Athletics U20 Championships in Nairobi, Kenya. Then came the COVID-19 pandemic. Like elsewhere in the world, COVID-19 caused severe limitations on athletes' training in Nigeria. Stadiums were locked down and athletes and coaches were not allowed to meet, so Endurance had to find a different way to conduct training sessions. "It was the first time I had to invent a way for us to train, making the best of a difficult situation to maintain fitness."

Endurance researched the internet for cross-training exercises, a training tool she had not previously paid much attention to. Encouraging her athletes to train at home using the material she had unearthed, she is convinced that their fitness now exceeds prepandemic standards. Nigerian attitudes presented a challenge. "Some people were so blind and deaf to what was happening. Where I come from, they don't believe there is such a thing as COVID-19 and so didn't take it seriously until the government got involved to the extent that people were told that those not wearing a face mask would be arrested. I really had an issue with people who refused to social distance. Nigerians are very stubborn; if you want to talk close to somebody, you just do."

Anticipating a Happy Future, Personally and Professionally

Endurance is keenly aware that her exposure to the world outside of Sapele has changed her. "I talk different, I act different, and I think different from most of the people I grew up with. Sometimes they tell me, when we meet and have a conversation and I open my mouth to speak, 'Endurance, you have been so exposed to the world, you have seen things that we have not seen, you reason differently from us.' But I try not to make them feel inferior."

Endurance speaks of her children with pride. Immanuela is studying for a master's degree in psychology at Arizona State University in Tempe. She was a European U-20 champion in 2019 and specialises in the 100 metres and 200 metres. Born in England, she grew up there, trained there, and competes for Britain. She aims to be the best athlete she can be and has said that her mother and coaches have a sense of how fast she can go. "My mum has said she sees me running faster than she did ... I have always relied on her knowledge with training programmes and strategies..." Edward is nine years old and attends primary school.

Endurance's family life changed dramatically when, in 2022, she found the strength to walk away from her unhappy marriage. And then, in December 2022, she married "the love of her life," Anthony (Tony) Ogheneyerowo Akpeki, in a traditional ceremony in Delta State. "I found happiness; he is very supportive of me, and he very much understands what it takes for me to be a good coach and produce great athletes."

Endurance added that her coaching career seems bright. The Athletics Federation of Nigeria (AFN) and the Nigeria Olympic Committee have shown their confidence in her abilities, nominating her for a 2024 Women in Sport High Performance Pathway (WISH)[41] scholarship in the United Kingdom. WISH is designed to support women coaches like Endurance in getting to the top level of coaching within their sport. "The one-week residential training felt like a lifetime of learning. What I gained in one week, some people spend a lifetime trying to achieve."

Endurance has indeed gained the recognition and support she deserves. "After the role I played through the WCIP, the AFN has more confidence in me; I try to better myself every opportunity I get to do so."

---

[41] Yemi Olus-Galadima, "How the IOC's WISH Programme for Female Coaches is Bridging the Gender Gap Ahead of Paris 2024," World Athletics, May 2, 2023, https://worldathletics.org/women-in-athletics/news/ioc-wish-programme-coaching-paris-2024.

Chapter Sixteen

Grace Mmolai

Botswana

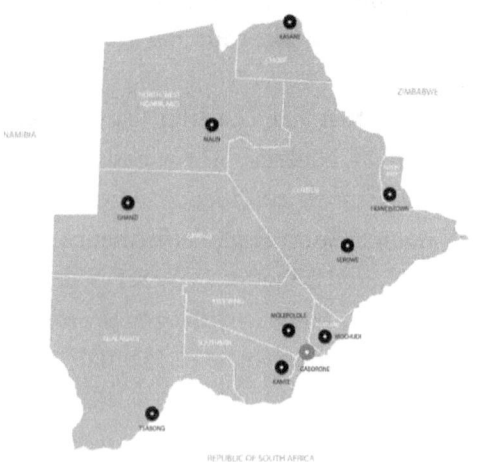

Serule is a small village in Botswana's Central District, some 340 kilometres northeast of the country's capital, Gaborone, and 87 kilometres from Francistown, its second largest city. It is home to around 3,000 people, mainly of four ethnicities: Bangwato, Bakwena, Bakalanga, and Bahurutshe. Most are farmers who depend on agriculture, while a significant number make a living from formal and informal employment within the village and in nearby urban areas. The population is served by a police station, a day care centre, a primary school, a clinic, a post office, and the Bonwatlou Community

Junior Secondary School, which provides education to learners from preprimary to secondary levels.

In recent years, Serule has experienced significant infrastructure growth. Housing is close to being on a par with urban dwellings, and most amenities are available.

Grace Mmolai, who teaches religious education at the school, noted that the growth includes water supply and transport systems and most services and facilities, although banking and shopping requires travel to the nearby centres of Selebi-Phikwe, Francistown, or Palapye.

The school is the hub of a thriving boxing club, the Bonwatlou JSS Boxing Club, the brainchild of Grace, a fiercely determined coach whose passion for boxing has attracted national and international attention. Boxing is a relatively new sport in Botswana, dating back only to the 1960s. The Botswana Boxing Association (BoBA) has reported a membership of just over 5,000 in a country with a population of about 2.5 million in 2023. Given the country's significant barriers to gender equality, it's rare for a Motswana[42] woman to achieve coaching success, especially one who, like Grace, lacks a boxing history.

Grace was born on April 6, 1984, in Francistown, to Florence Lola Nzala Matlho and Dr. Steven Ludick Klinc. She has three brothers — Tebogo Ryan, Tshepiso KingZee, and George — and had one sister, the late Tina Olga. KingZee lives in Francistown, George lives in Gaborone, and Tebogo lives with his wife and children in Tonota, about 40 miles north of Serule. Grace's mother passed away in 2011; her father lives in Gaborone, but he and Grace are not on good terms and do not keep in contact.

Grace remembers her childhood in Francistown as a happy time thanks to Florence, who raised her children as a single mother while working as a supermarket supervisor. "She provided anything and everything for us; she educated us and offered us the best, so we never struggled."

---

[42] Motswana: a member of the Tswana people or a person from Botswana.

184   Stories of Resilience and Courage

Grace Mmolai

Grace's large extended family includes grandparents, aunties, and cousins and she was always included in gatherings and activities. "There was a division of duties, and everyone had a role to play. That brought unity and stability and love and attention. We were always there for each other."

Living on an Ancient Land

Botswana is one of Africa's oldest democracies. Its economy focuses on diamond mining and tourism. It has a high standard of education, which is free and compulsory for the first ten years. Primary school consists of Grades 1 to 7 for children ages six to thirteen; junior secondary school covers the next three years; and senior secondary school is of a two-year duration.

Grace's schooling began with kindergarten in 1987, followed by Our Lady of the Desert Primary School in 1991, Mmei Junior Secondary School in 1998, and then Francistown Senior Secondary School. In 2003, she entered the University of Botswana in Gaborone but, because of her passion for working with children, switched to Tonota College of Education in Greater Francistown, graduating in 2007.

Leaving home and living in a hostel was difficult for Grace. "I was leaving my family behind, and I had never lived away from them. I had to learn to be independent, which required a lot of responsibility and accountability on my part. When I graduated, I was ready to face society and handle the challenges and hardships that come with adulthood."

Reminiscing about her childhood, Grace remembers primary school for its eight-hour days and moving from teacher to teacher depending upon the subject. She had many favourites, including mathematics, Setswana (the Bantu language of the Tswana people), social studies, sciences, art, history, and religious education. "You can imagine how exhausting it is to pay attention for so long."

Grace looked forwards to extracurricular activities, such as sports and clubs, which offered the opportunity to relax with friends. "I loved to meet people, to interact with the different personalities, to see what people are like outside of the classroom. Inside the classroom, we always tried to be so serious, but when you are outside you can be free-spirited and be yourself. That was the part I loved; I always became me, that loud, extroverted person, the person with so much energy."

Traditional games were a favourite after-school activity and included Black Mampatile (a Tswana version of hide-and-seek) and Koi, a group rope game often accompanied by rhythmic chants. Games were acceptable for both genders, but when Grace was growing up, only athletics and tennis were considered appropriate sports for girls. Later, football gained acceptance and, as befitted a person in a football-mad country, Grace played the game throughout her youth, adding basketball during her college years.

Botswana's Traditional Games

"Like any Tswana child," Grace said, "I played all these games."

Mhele — A board game similar to chess.

Mantlwane — A role-playing game with houses carved out of clay. Kids even pretend to cook real food for the "family."

Suna Baby — A dodgeball-type game using balls made of plastic bags or stockings.

Skonti Bolo/Sewerewere — In this hide-and-seek game, the seeker also has to guard a ball. The hiders can sneak out and kick the ball from its spot, and then the seeker must restart their search for everyone in the game. This can go on for hours or even a whole day.

Diketo — This game is similar to Jacks. Players throw pebbles into the air while simultaneously sweeping other pebbles into several holes in the ground.

Molao Molao — Players agree that whenever they call each other's name, the other will answer "Molao." If they don't answer correctly, the caller can decree a one-time temporary law, such as "Go get me some water" or even "You have to give me your food for the day."

Ke Dutse — This means "I am seated." Players agree to each announce, "I'm sitting" whenever they take a seat. If they don't say this, they may be slapped across the face, usually when they don't expect it.

The games vary by name and rules depending on region of the country.

A Love Affair with Boxing

At the age of sixteen, Grace realised that boxing was her passion — not that she had herself boxed or even seen a live match. In fact, television provided her only exposure to the sport. "Funnily enough, there was something about it. I would stay up until two a.m. waiting for the matches to be aired, sometimes live, sometimes re-runs, including Muhammad Ali, his opponents. I didn't miss a match."

Grace has always been attracted by the discipline and passion boxers display in the ring, and she associates life realities with boxing and its similarity to everyday situations. "Life is like a boxing ring. You go in there and either you get knocked down or you stand up for yourself and try again. If you don't get up, that's the end of you ... Boxing gives a child a life scenario, the reality that life is. When they go out into the world, becoming part of the community as responsible citizens, they will face difficulties, failure, disappointment; being in the ring teaches them how to cope and become someone in life."

Grace's teaching career began in 2008, when the government, as is the policy, posted her to Bonwatlou Community Junior Secondary School in Serule. The 670 students, ages twelve to eighteen years old, came from six nearby villages. From the beginning, her duties included coaching a girls' football team, but by 2010, she developed an interest in bringing boxing to the school. Although she lacked coaching credentials, she approached school management with a proposal: "I really want to try to build a girls' boxing team, as they have none. Give me a chance to coach six girls and six boys from the school." She explained that boxing must be in her blood from having watched so much of it and, she pointed out, she was the only member of her family to love the sport. "My father was a good karateka but, since he and I were not on good terms, I never did karate."

Once Grace's request was granted, she set out on what would be a life-changing path. Proceeding cautiously, she waited until 2012 to enter her twelve prospects in competitions and celebrated when their results exceeded expectations. "They won the subzonals, the zonals, and the nationals. That's where I got my twelve gold medals!" By 2013, the twelve comprised the best secondary school team in Botswana and had the trophy to prove it.

In 2015, the Botswana Boxing Association chose Grace to coach at the Botswana Games, a national multisport event launched in 2005 to prepare young athletes (nineteen years and under) for international multisport competitions, such as the Olympics, the Commonwealth Games, the African Union Sports Council Region 5 Under-20 Youth Games, and the All-Africa Games.

Again, Grace's boxers shone, winning numerous medals. Their success ignited the BoBA's interest in her, and the association made it possible for her to attain the International Boxing Association's Star 1 Coaching Certification by sending her to Zambia in 2017 for the course. She remains Botswana's only female certified boxing coach.

As Grace's coaching reputation grew, so did her family responsibilities. In 2012, she married Alfred Mmolai, a plant mechanical engineer who works at a diamond mine in the north of the country and returns home to Serule on his days off. They divorced in 2022. They are the parents of Mildred, born in 2006, and Cecilia, born in 2009. Initially, Alfred was not supportive of Grace's coaching, mainly because of her constant travel to interschool competitions throughout Botswana. "I was always on the move, but I never left him with the kids; they always came with me, wherever I went." For the most part, Grace was able to rely on her extended family for accommodations when on the road. And when that wasn't possible, she and her daughters and often the boxers would sleep in a classroom. "Wherever the team was camping out, I was there with my kids. Having them with me was an accepted situation, and the school authorities were very accommodating." Nowadays, her daughters, who have developed into good boxers, accept Grace's commitments and simply wave good-bye.

Even though her one hour and fifty minutes of coaching takes place each day after eight hours of teaching, Grace's passion has not waned. She brings the instincts and training of a teacher to her methodology: Rather than emphasising competitions and winning, Grace focuses on developing her boxers as people. "Sport is not at all about competing. It's about you gaining the confidence to face the world and be yourself, not what someone else wants you to be." She compares coaching to parenting, which to her means providing opportunities to explore what the boxers love and learning their strengths and weaknesses. "I ask them: 'What are you willing to learn from what I offer as a coach?' It's about walking with them until they are ready to walk on their own. That's how I get my boxers to love what I do with them."

Not surprisingly, Grace often encounters parents who view with trepidation their child's passion for boxing, assuming they will be getting a beating. She counters their concerns with education to sensitise and create awareness of the value of the sport in helping to develop contributing members of society. "During prize-giving, parents see their child being rewarded for their good work. They watch boxers demonstrate the sport and learn what it is all about. Because I engage them, I am very much supported by parents."

To train, Grace makes do with the barest of necessities. Lacking a gym, she will use a classroom, the generator room, a hallway, whatever is available. Chairs create the boundaries of a ring, so the boxers develop an understanding of its dimensions. "When it's training time, we train, no matter what. Even with our limitations, they excel at big competitions, but I am struggling." Travel to competitions is usually by bus, and luckily the school pays for fares and food. Accommodation is whatever is available.

Equipment is another challenge. Supplied by the Ministry of Education, each school receives around CAD$1,135 annually to be allocated among all the sports it supports. Grace may get nothing or, if lucky, two pairs of gloves for a team of fifteen boxers. She does get mouth guards each year; however, the lack of equipment makes competing difficult. "When we go to competitions, the boxers share gloves, boots, everything because they don't have personal equipment. I have three red vests, three red shorts ... If you wear a size five shoe, you have a problem, because I only have sizes six and seven. And this in a prosperous country! To overcome these challenges, one has to keep pleading with the ministry to purchase more resources."

WCIP: A Once-in-a-Lifetime Opportunity

Participating in the Women Coach Internship Programme developed by the Commonwealth Games Federation for the 2018 Commonwealth Games in Gold Coast, Australia, may have seemed like an unlikely opportunity for Grace, living as she does away from Botswana's sporting mainstream. Still, when her friend Healer, who knew of her talent for developing young boxers, encouraged her to apply, Grace submitted her application to the Botswana National Olympic Committee along with a letter of recommendation from him. Acceptance led to her first trip out of Africa. Her husband was unavailable to care for the children because of his distant workplace, so Grace turned to her daughters' grandmother and aunt, who agreed to stay with them for the duration of her absence.

Grace returned home, affirmed by the WCIP experience as a woman and as a coach. "I can say proudly that I am a coach, and I don't need to be reminded all the time of my gender. I learned that I had to sell my sport and myself to get support from the community and the media. I am a coach and I have potential and I can produce results if given the opportunity. As a woman, I can compete with the world if given the chance. And if given the chance, I will grab it!"

She is still waiting for that chance. Lack of utilisation of her skills by the BoBA stings, even though every year she coaches her boxers to the national level. In 2021, for example, fuelled by determination and optimism despite her challenges, she took six female and five male boxers to the national youth championships where they won two gold, five silver, and four bronze medals. Her only coaching assignment since the WCIP was as part of a team training boxers for the 2019 African Union Sports Council Region 5 Youth Games. On another occasion, she heard that she had been named to coach at a regional event, but official confirmation never came. "Truth be told, the BoBA has not talked to me about anything nor have they invited me to any events, so I have decided to concentrate on and push my passion for developing young boxers."

One important consequence of the WCIP was Grace's commitment to being a role model for her female boxers. "Don't look up to men; look up to me as a woman standing before you, saying you can succeed if you believe in yourself as a girl-child." She also decided to make coaching her female boxers a priority. "We need to be a voice for girls and empower them. They have potential, just like male athletes."

Grace with her mentor, Luca Lechedanzi, at the WCIP closing reception
Photographer: Murray Rix, Rix Ryan Photography Qld. Supplied by Griffith Uni Gold Coast, Queensland.

Meeting the Challenges of COVID-19

Botswana's Public Health Act, along with the Emergency Powers Act, which was implemented April 2020 to address the pandemic, promptly provided the framework for a response before a case reached Botswana's borders. Importantly, this included closing the borders. The first lockdown began on April 2, 2020, after a case was reported in late March and the government declared a state of emergency. In May 2020, schools began to reopen with new sanitary measures in place, including social distancing and wearing masks. In 2021, WHO and the Government of Botswana began a national communication campaign with a focus on the importance of social measures.

COVID-19 brought sport activities to a halt, with officials concentrating on preparing for the 2020 Olympic Games in Tokyo (delayed until 2021), and nothing else. "The worst was at first when we didn't know what was happening. Then I gave my boxers training programmes to do at home or in a hostel; some of my boxers are boarders. By 2021, I was allowed to train them individually and tried for thirty minutes a day, along with having them train on their own. We wore masks and tried to distance as much as possible."

Looking Ahead

Grace pins her hopes on one day having a gym room and being in charge of her own club. Her twin passions remain female empowerment through boxing and developing young boxers of both genders. If ever given the opportunity to coach the national team, she would accept, but that is not a goal. All she wants is to be recognised as a coach. "The [BoBA] paid for me to acquire the coaching credentials to coach nationally and internationally, so why are they not utilising me? That is a worry.

"I stand for what I believe in and will keep doing my best in any opportunity I am given in boxing. My quest for success means producing boxers for the national team. My passion is fuelled by determination and optimism despite the challenges I encounter."

Chapter Seventeen

Amanda Murphy
New Zealand

Amanda Murphy is one of those rare woman athletes to have worn the treasured jersey of New Zealand's Black Ferns, known worldwide as one of rugby's premier sides: Olympic champions at Tokyo 2020, six-time winners of the Women's Rugby World Cup[43] (in 1998, 2002,

---

[43] In 2019, in an effort to promote gender equality, World Rugby announced that, beginning in 2021, the women's championship would officially have the same name as the men's: Rugby World Cup.

2006, 2010, 2017, and 2021), and silver medallists at the 2016 Rio Olympics.

Like so many New Zealand youngsters, Amanda began playing rugby at the age of five, continued throughout her secondary school years, and earned a coveted spot on the Black Ferns in 2009 at the age of twenty-four. Since retiring in 2013, she has filled several positions with the celebrated squad and is currently its lead strength and conditioning coach.

Sport has always figured prominently in Amanda's life, both as an athlete and a coach, in and out of school, organised and impromptu. She was born on September 20, 1985, in Invercargill/Waihōpai,[44] the regional capital and commercial hub of Southland, to teenagers who placed her for adoption when she was ten days old. "I became part of another family, which was — and is — awesome." Her family consists of parents Michael and Gail; brother David, born in 1987; sister Amiria, born in 1988; and brother Simon, born in 1992. In 2010, Amanda met her birth mother and is connected with her birth father and his family.

When Amanda was a toddler, the family left Invercargill/Waihōpai for Geraldine/Heratini, a pretty country village 440 kilometres to the north on the Waihi River, in the heart of a prosperous farming area that is well known for its artists and crafts people. Even small places like Geraldine offer a wide range of sporting opportunities for youngsters. During her primary and secondary schooling, Amanda, a natural athlete, played rugby, cricket, and athletics and dabbled in badminton, basketball, and netball. "Hayden, my best mate, lived just up the road. He played Rugby Union, and I wanted to be like him, so I played too. And most days, I would be out on our large back lawn with my brother, David, and I couldn't wait to line him up. I'd ask him to run straight at me.[45] More often than not,

---

[44] In the 1920s, New Zealand began giving some places two names; this tradition was seen more often in the 1990s and 2000s, partly because of the Treaty of Waitangi settlements.
[45] A Kiwi expression: When someone has a rugby ball and sprints into another individual who yells, "Run it straight!"

he came off second best, but now he is bigger and stronger, so I don't know that I would challenge him anymore."

As Amanda reflects on her happy childhood, two memories stand out: how well sport was organised and the strong connection she developed with Doug Bruce, her form teacher in Year 6 and a former All Black, which is a player on the New Zealand national rugby union team. "Having an ex–All Black as your teacher for a year, how good was that! We had a natural connection and understood each other, and absolutely he was a mentor. It was he who dubbed me 'Smurf,' a nickname that has stuck." Years later, the two caught up, and Amanda was delighted that Doug had followed her career and knew she had become a Black Fern.

Throughout secondary school, Amanda had no specific goals. "I was cruising, just doing what I felt like doing on any given day. It's coulda, woulda, shoulda; my life could have been completely different." In 2004, right out of school, she joined the New Zealand Defence Force as a firefighter. Years earlier, her mother had predicted a military career. Amanda says that, at the time, her reaction was a vehement, "No, I won't. I'll never do that. I later realised that, when told I can't, I find a way. I don't know why Mom said that. Maybe because I was always out building tree huts, digging, and helping Dad. I certainly wasn't a girly girl; I was always trying to beat the boys. And I love challenges, and Mom saw that. Even at an early age, I wanted to be the best all the time."

Firefighting appealed because Amanda enjoyed helping people and being on a team, and she was attracted by the physical side of the profession. "The highlights of this experience would be the close-knit team and learnings you can take with you wherever you go. I have a love of learning and finding ways to achieve better results."

On Becoming a Black Fern

In 2007, at the age of twenty-two, Amanda left the military and crossed the Tasman Sea to Brisbane, Australia, prompted by the urge to find a new direction and explore more of the world. She had loved her time in the military but, liking change and feeling she needed it, she heeded her instincts. "I had just got out of the military, where life was so structured. I woke up on a Sunday morning, booked my flight, and was gone within a few days. I had no plan but wanted to experience what life in Australia was like. Get out of New Zealand basically."

Amanda Murphy

The move signalled a turning point in Amanda's relationship with rugby. While she possessed natural athletic ability, which brought her to a certain level of expertise in several sports, until this point, she lacked direction and purpose. Once settled in Brisbane, she joined a club rugby team and also played for the State of Queensland.

"Playing for Canterbury in New Zealand is the equivalent of playing for Queensland in Australia. I had played for Canterbury [a region of South Island] for a few years, so I would say it was on par with the level I was at." So, when a teammate insisted that she could make any team she wanted if she actually gave it a shot and did the work, she paid attention.

Amanda also paid attention when a coach suggested she play rugby for Australia, if not in the way the coach intended. "If you're a Kiwi, you strive to play for the Fern!" So, after one year in Brisbane, she packed her bags and headed home to Christchurch/Ōtautahi. Knowing that a close friend, Halie Hurring, had just been named to the Black Ferns triggered her own ambition. "I thought, right, let's have a go." Following seven months of formalised training and a positional change from centre to blindside flanker,[46] she had her own Black Fern jersey. "You can cruise or you can do something about it and get it done. You get out what you put in."

Amanda's career with the Black Ferns ran from 2009 to the end of 2012. A highlight came in 2011 when, wearing her treasured jersey, she ran out before a full crowd to challenge England at the prestigious Twickenham Stoop Stadium. Unfortunately for the Ferns, the Red Roses registered a 10–3 maiden victory. But even more than that moment, surreal as it was, the most important aspect of her Black Fern experience were the friendships she made and the bonds she formed. "That's the biggest impact sport has had on me. And it has allowed me to be me, to be my authentic self, and to do what I love to do." Unfortunately, serious injuries interfered with her playing career, including one to her ACL, a common knee injury. Surgery forced her to miss the 2010 World Cup and, in 2011, she ruptured the pectoralis major tendon, an uncommon injury, but one that can result in significant disability.

"Although my injuries were major, I just kept getting up. Everyone goes through rough times, and you've just got to keep

---

[46] A blindside flanker is a forward who lines up at the back of the scrum with the openside flanker and the number eight. The term flanker originates from the players' positions — they flank each set of forwards.

going. I learned resilience and I had a decent amount of that anyway; otherwise, I wouldn't have done it. But eventually I decided to hang my boots up and retire from rugby. I wanted another challenge. As a teenager, I was quite good at javelin so thought I'd have another nudge and started training in 2013, tapping into the High Performance Sport New Zealand transfer programme." This initiative helps high performance athletes from one sport transfer into another targeted sport by recognising physical attributes that may lead to success in the new sport, given time and support.

No surprise, Amanda's goal was to become the best thrower possible, to see how far she could get, with the 2018 Commonwealth Games in mind. "Being the best is always in the forefront of my mind, regardless of whether it be work or sport or relationships or family." In 2016, she moved to Perth, Australia, "to give it a hot crack" and train with Kim Mickle, one of the region's best throwers, but success wasn't to be; her body had sustained too many rugby injuries. "My arm doesn't straighten, I'm a walking mess, and I was trying to compete against people who are unrestricted, so that was the end of that. The question was, what am I going to do next?"

Coaching Takes Hold

Amanda had realised that there were gaps in her formal education, so in 2011, while recuperating from her knee surgery, she decided to polish her academic and coaching credentials, planning to combine the two into a professional career. First, she took a personal training course at the Southern Institute of Technology, Christchurch Campus. She then went to Hamilton/Kirikiriroa (a city on the North Island) to study exercise science and to supplement the Level 2 Coach Accreditation course and other courses she completed while in Perth through the Australian Strength and Conditioning Association and with Athletics Australia. She added a bachelor of sport and exercise science from the Waikato Institute of Technology, also in Hamilton/Kirikiriroa, and a bachelor of applied science from the Christchurch Polytechnic Institute of Technology.

Coaching had long been an interest. For Amanda, it was a natural offshoot from her passion for strength and conditioning, and as early as 2010, she had begun to coach the Canterbury Secondary School Girls team in Christchurch/Ōtautahi.

In 2017, unable to realise her javelin dream, Amanda returned to New Zealand with Kim, who was now her life partner, and settled in Christchurch/Ōtautahi. Amanda had lived nearby while serving with the military at Burnham Military Camp, the largest on the South Island and 28 kilometres south of Christchurch/Ōtautahi. At first, she worked for the Canterbury School District, coaching a secondary school rugby team. She then took a job with Athletics New Zealand (ANZ) as a high performance assistant throws coach in its Christchurch/Ōtautahi unit. She developed personal training clients, and that stimulated her hunger to help people. She added an internship at the Christchurch-based Crusaders International Academy, which delivers rugby skills training for female and male athletes.

Over time, Amanda progressed to close to full-time coaching for ANZ. "I was really, really happy in my workplace. Things were great, loved it." In the meantime, the growth of women's rugby globally prompted the New Zealand Rugby Union to fund women's coaching in its provinces, one of which is Canterbury. The Canterbury Rugby Football Union (CRFU) responded by creating the following roles: women's high performance manager and women's lead strength and conditioning coach. Although she was happy coaching athletics, rugby remained Amanda's passion, so she decided to "chuck [her] name in the hat." Given her experience, she felt she had as good a chance as any of being the successful applicant.

As busy as she was, Amanda leapt at the opportunity to apply for a spot with the Women Coach Internship Programme at the 2018 Commonwealth Games in Gold Coast, Australia. She became one of three Kiwis — the others were Victoria Grant (Chapter Two) and Cordelia Norris (Chapter Nine) — to be accepted into the twenty-intern programme. During the Games, she gained firsthand experience of what is required of a coach at a multisport event.

"It was an awesome opportunity, really great preparation for future coaching at the international level. Looking back, I struggled with being around other people constantly and recognised that I need to step back and take time out for myself and be alone in a quiet room. It's a learning I have applied ever since, getting away from everyone and recharging the batteries. This has had quite an impact on me…"

Amanda's application for the CRFU rugby job was accepted after she agreed to include a strength and conditioning role. Unwilling to sever her ties with the ANZ — "I was absolutely happy there" — she became a volunteer coach. Her partner, Kim, moved from volunteering to become assistant coach, focusing on throws. "She's a much better thrower than I ever was, so I just assist when I can."

In her role with the CRFU, Amanda oversaw the province's women's high performance Academy programme in which eight semiprofessional athletes, who are also on the Black Ferns roster, were enrolled. Another twenty athletes played for the Canterbury regional team. The programme provides the women with mental skills training, nutritional information, strength and conditioning, technical and tactical skills, and well-being and personal development. "The programme is phenomenal, and it keeps getting better and better."

Constantly Extending Her Boundaries

Amanda has always dreamt big, and she's not about to stop. As noted, she is "extremely goal-oriented," with an overarching ambition to be the best she can be and to leave a legacy that focuses around giving people opportunities, especially girls and women. "I dream big. I dream massive. Throw something out there, and I'm not afraid if it doesn't happen the way I want it, because I know another door is going to open. If I fall, I get back up, and I want people I coach and work with to do the same. Just keep going.

"Growing up, I was always wanting to be better. I do have dreams, but they are really loose. Right now, I have a lot of freedom and flexibility and, if I really want to do something, I'll set a plan and do it a hundred and ten per cent. I'm an all or nothing being."

What Amanda — and millions of others — could never have anticipated was the worldwide pandemic, COVID-19, which struck in 2019. As noted in Chapter Nine, the New Zealand government reacted quickly and imposed multiple lockdowns and other restrictions between February 2020 to September 2022.

Amanda notes that, compared with many of the world's nations, New Zealand was fortunate. For her, the plus side to the pandemic is that it afforded a rare opportunity to relax. "The first three weeks after the World Health Organization declared a pandemic, and certainly it was true for the athletes I was looking after, everyone was, 'Oh, we get to have a break.' Then COVID-19 arrived in the country, and you wondered if it was ever going to end. Basically, we lived a normal life aside from not being able to do any international travel. We were incredibly lucky and I'm very grateful. Prime Minister Jacinda Ardern did a bloody good job, and we were also incredibly lucky geographically."

During this period, Amanda came full circle with the Black Ferns. "I've worn the jersey and I want to help those wearing the jersey and those who want to wear the jersey to improve and challenge the norm." In 2019, opportunity knocked, taking her from player to a dream position as strength and conditioning coach (Black Ferns Development) to strength and conditioning coach (Black Ferns Probables) in 2020. She then became the Black Ferns assistant strength and conditioning coach in 2022 and the lead strength and conditioning coach in 2023. In accepting the latter appointment, Amanda moved on from the CRFU after four productive years in which its women's programmes grew, as did she.

What's Next?

As for her future, Amanda has no idea what lies around the corner. "When I moved to Perth, I thought, I'm here, and here I'm staying. Only one year later, I was shipping out the door to work with ANZ, then CRFU and the Black Ferns. And now I'm with the Black Ferns, my passion — and my pathway.

"My family have always been supportive of my dreams and goals, as wild as they have been. They are extremely proud of my journey and know how much time, work, and dedication it has taken for me to be in the position I am. It's surreal for a little girl from a small town in New Zealand to be living her dream every day."

Amanda brings passion and knowledge to her coaching.

Chapter Eighteen

Sheila Gakii

Kenya

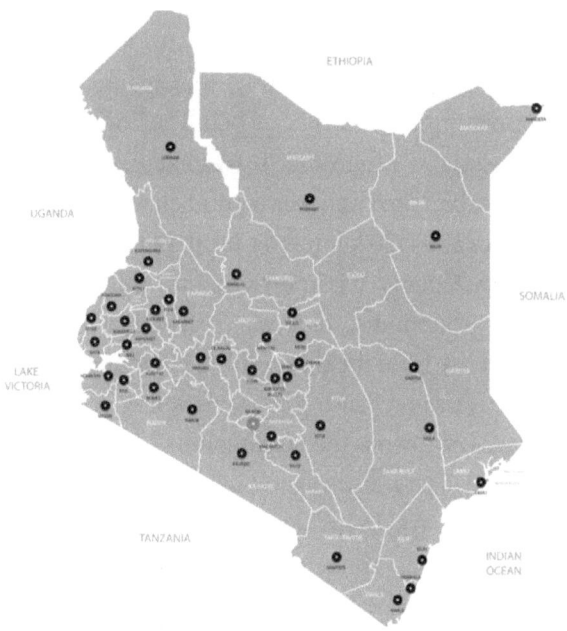

An unsettled childhood and a challenging adulthood haven't prevented Sheila Gakii from making significant inroads to becoming one of Kenya's promising young badminton coaches.

The youngest of three children, Sheila was born on April 4, 1992, in Meru, a farming community some 230 kilometres northeast of

Nairobi, Kenya's capital. Nairobi is a teeming metropolis of over 5 million people and is the hub of government, industry, and tourism with its incredible wildlife preserves, transportation, health services, education, and communication. Meru, with a population of just under 1.5 million, is a busy business, agricultural, and educational centre that produces coffee, tea, timber, macadamia nuts, mangoes, and dairy products.

Sheila's father and her mother, Fedis Kaari Kibii, were teachers who separated when she was very young. The premature death of Fedis, when Sheila was five or so years old, left her and her siblings — Wayne Mureithi and Jean Makena — in the care of her grandmother, Eileen Kibei, for the next three years. At the age of ten, Sheila moved to Kakamega to live with her aunt, Millicent Ntue Kibii, and to continue her education. Her father is estranged from his children and was not involved in their upbringing.

"My aunt took over because she had no kids of her own and wanted to help my grandmother, who was ageing. Also, Kakamega had more opportunities in terms of better schools. Wayne was the first to move; Jean and I followed. It was exciting to move from the rural area to an urban area and was a good change of scenery."

Kakamega lies about 30 kilometres north of the equator. The largest town in Kakamega County, it is known for bull fighting and agriculture, including maize, groundnuts, sugarcane, tea, and traditional vegetables. Many people here are from the Luhya tribe. Their main way of earning a living is cash crop farming. Raising chickens is also an integral part of the Luhya economy. The town is the headquarters of Mumias Sugar, one of Kenya's largest sugar-processing companies.

Despite the upheaval in her family life, Sheila described herself as "a normal African child." She said, "I went to school, I did chores such as cleaning the one-bedroom house with a kitchen, toilet, bathroom, a small compound, and a garden where we planted vegetables like kales, bananas, and potatoes for family use. I also did the dishes but not the cooking; that didn't start until I was in secondary school."

Sheila's early education began in Meru at Kariakomo Primary School. She then progressed to Butere Girls High School, a four-year institution where she began to study mass communications in hopes of becoming a publicist or a public relations specialist.

When she was fourteen, Sheila took up badminton, which started in secondary school. Initially interested in playing basketball, she was persuaded by badminton coach George Mukabi to give the sport a try, even though she had never played it. Impressed by her natural talent, Mukabi, who also taught history and geography at the school, insisted that she continue, convinced that she had a future in competitive badminton. "I never imagined I could do that until I started beating my older teammates who had played longer. I was very skinny and tall, which is an advantage in badminton because it makes movement easier. Also, I have always been naturally energetic, so it was easy to adjust to the game. Mentally, I was very strong because I believed I was the best and so had no fear of failure."

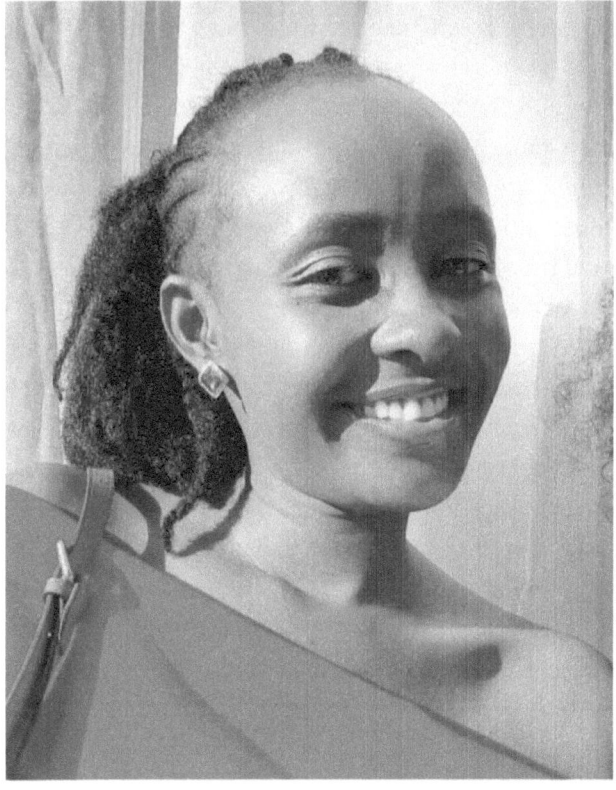

Sheila Gakii

Becoming an International Player

Connecting with Mukabi marked the beginning of a journey that gave Sheila many opportunities in a sport that remains an essential part of her life. That she progressed so far was due largely to her aunt Millicent. "She raised me and supported me all through my badminton journey, paid my school fees, and ensured I was well taken care of." At the age of fifteen, Mukabi sent Sheila to the Kenya National School Games Championships where she won the first of four consecutive singles titles. The encouragement he provided was constant throughout her secondary school years and was a factor in her excellent results in singles, doubles, and mixed doubles. She was also inspired by the fact that, even though her school's court was outdoors, its players still managed to win trophies and medals at the championships, which are designed to nurture talented secondary school students.

In 2008, the sixteen-year-old was named to the Kenyan national badminton team and straightaway competed at the Youth Commonwealth Games in Pune, India. Although she lost in the first round, the Games were an important learning experience. "It was very different from secondary school competitions where I just played other students. At that time, I didn't have the kind of professional training you get as a national team player."

Sheila acknowledged that she was fortunate the Kenyan education system allows, even encourages, students to participate in sports and to reach the highest level they can. For her, the national championships and the Commonwealth Youth Games were the pinnacle of her ten-year career. Importantly, the system taught her that sport and education are of equal value.

Sheila's experience in Pune led to her move to Nairobi in 2009 to train with John Odhiambo, the head coach at the Kenya Badminton Association (KBA), who became her mentor. During her time on the national team, she competed at the 2011 All-Africa Games, making it to the quarterfinals. Living in Nairobi was expensive, especially for a young athlete who was also a university student, and it would have been unmanageable, but she was able to stay with her aunt Millicent and aunt Emily Gatakaa (who has since passed away), and later with her aunt Assenath Wanja. "Badminton is not supported by the government; everything has to come out of your own pocket. As well as paying my coaching fees, my family also paid for me to play in local tournaments, which you have to do in order to get seeded for international tournaments, such as the Mombasa Open Tournament, the Kisumu Open, the Eldoret Open, and the Jamuhuri Open. So they paid for me to play, to travel, for accommodations, equipment, shoes — everything."

The 2011 All-Africa Games were the highlight of Sheila's competitive career. "Reaching the quarterfinals with my partner, Mercy Joseph, was such a big achievement. We gave the Nigerian team, who were older and more experienced than us, a run for their money. The game went up to three sets. We won the first and they won the second and the third."

Sheila retired shortly after that, when she became pregnant with her son, Griffin Wogute, who was born on December 13, 2013. Although she tried coming back after the pregnancy, it was made difficult by financial and time constraints. It was at this time that she opted for coaching.

Sheila's interest in coaching grew as she realised that she had the talent and skills to help younger students discover and develop their potential. Kenya lacked a woman badminton coach, and she believed that if she "filled those shoes," she could foster talent development at the grassroots and primary school levels, especially where young girls were concerned. Before long, she started assisting Odhiambo. "It was a way to earn some money, but mostly I enjoyed watching people learn the sport and wanted to guide other players in whichever way I could; I thought coaching would help me to make a difference. I wanted to put Kenya on the badminton map, but that proved to be hard because it is an expensive sport, and you are often forced to work only with those who can afford it. Government funding is minimal and training facilities are hard to come by."

To gain coaching credentials, in 2012 Sheila completed the Badminton World Federation (BWF) Level 1 course in Cairo, Egypt.

Odhiambo continued to provide guidance, teaching her coaching techniques and how to recognise and develop a player's strengths and identify and overcome weaknesses. Also encouraging Sheila's coaching aspirations were Jeff Shigoli (Badminton Kenya's secretary-general) and Anna Maina (former chair of the KBA), who encouraged her to enrol in various coaching and administration courses, including a course in badminton administration in Addis Ababa, Ethiopia, and another sponsored by the NOCK, also in Ethiopia.

The latter courses inspired her to establish the Badminton Women's Commission. The intent was to empower women with a long history in the sport to encourage other women to continue playing after finishing university. This in turn led her to apply to be a delegate to a Women and Empowerment Conference in Nairobi in 2019. "I was the most qualified candidate because I had formed the commission, was a member of the KBA, had management experience, and was prepared to work with the NOCK. Learnings included guidance on doping, dealing with sexual harassment, and pushing forwards to break barriers that prevent women from leadership positions. It was clear that we must be ready to fight for our seat at the big table and fight all that is thrown our way."

During this time, Sheila was working towards a degree in mass communications with a specialisation in public relations at the Multimedia University of Kenya, but her family stopped supporting her and with the birth of Griffin, unable to pay the fees, she discontinued her schooling and turned her attention to carving out a coaching career and building a leadership role in Kenyan sport. These were unusual career goals for a Kenyan woman. "I wanted to be one of the few women running sports in my country. We have a shortage of women coaches and leaders in badminton, and I figured that coaching was a good start towards leadership. Most female players quit the sport after having children, and I wanted to hold on and encourage others."

Sheila Gakii spoke at a Women in Sports empowerment conference.

WCIP Growth Opportunity

At the suggestion of the NOCK, the KBA nominated Sheila for the Women Coach Internship Programme. Sheila, still one of Kenya's top players at the time, was also in the running for the one spot the KBA was allotting to a woman at the Games. Her WCIP candidacy was boosted by her coaching certification courses and, when notified the day before the trials that her application was successful, she was both excited and relieved. "I was favouring coaching over playing and so I hadn't been competing at local tournaments, which meant I hadn't accumulated enough points to earn me a good starting position at the trials. Being accepted for the WCIP meant I didn't need to compete, and I think coaching was the better path for me to follow."

Sheila benefitted from hearing the stories of her fellow intern coaches. She noted several common denominators: passion for their sport, passion for coaching, and similar problems regardless of where they lived in the Commonwealth. "We come from different sports and backgrounds, but we have so much in common. It was very inspiring how determined they are to deal with problems rather than letting the issues break them."

Sheila's experience at the Games was unique in that her mentor coach, John Odhiambo, was unable to travel to Gold Coast because of last-minute budget cuts. Always resourceful, she contacted Gilbert Ofuyuru, the coach of the Ugandan team, who suggested that she shadow him throughout the competition. The arrangement ensured that she was able to meet one of the WCIP requirements: that the intern coach be embedded with her team and have access to the field of play. She learned firsthand the role and responsibilities of a head coach during an international event and credited the Ugandan team with being accommodating and welcoming. She noted that having to make her own way contributed to her personal and professional growth. "The experience went well because I succeeded in getting myself a mentor coach. Learning from Gilbert was a plus. As the only Kenyan badminton coach, I was able to coach the men's singles game, but our one female player bowed out of the tournament because of an injury.

"I learned that coaching is about more than developing skills in your athletes. It's about partnership, encouragement, mental growth, and finding ways to improve yourself as a coach. I was reminded that coaching is a journey that requires a relationship and willingness on the part of both coach and athlete."

Upon her return to Kenya, Sheila was appointed to the NOCK Youth Development Commission. It is a point of pride that she was its youngest member. The commission scouts and develops talent in youth under the age of seventeen throughout the country and finds suitable coaches and facilities. "This was a major milestone for me as a young coach given my interest in developing a junior badminton team and preparing them for eventual Olympic competition." Determined to demonstrate that her appointment was on merit, Sheila was resourceful in presenting creative ideas, managing budgets, and planning youth camps. Unfortunately, her term was not renewed after Badminton Kenya was suspended indefinitely in March 2021 by the BWF and subsequently banned from competing at tournaments whether local, national, or international. The suspension, which came about after "incessant wrangles between rival factions battling for recognition,"⁴⁷ meant that Badminton Kenya could not vote at BWF general meetings, receive funding or membership grants, or enter players in competitions. "We are working towards an official election with the help of NOCK in August 2023, and then badminton in Kenya will return to normalcy."

Her disappointment at leaving the commission aside, Sheila notes that the WCIP changed her life and reinforced her determination to pursue a sports career. "It opened my eyes to the different opportunities and possibilities out there and helped me to meet Kenyan sports leaders who listened to my ideas and thoughts and suggested I could be an effective mentor for youth. It gave me the confidence to keep pushing forwards as a coach and sportswoman."

Sheila made it her life goal to establish a sports academy using the knowledge she gained from the WCIP and the contacts she made while with the commission. She envisioned a countrywide reach for the academy, which she planned to staff with trained coaches, many of whom would be women. They would create networks, brainstorm ideas, and achieve goals. "Sports academies in Kenya focus mainly on football, and it is my goal to revolutionise all sports and give them value. However , getting funding and facilities for this will take a while, and so I am starting with badminton as I work towards introducing myself to other coaches. I know the challenges coaches and players face and so I would be well positioned to mitigate them. I want all sports in the academy, but definitely tennis, table tennis, squash, and badminton, of course."

And then came COVID-19.

COVID-19: A Disruptive Force

As noted in Chapter Ten, Kenya's first case of COVID-19 was reported in March 2020. The country experienced several waves of the pandemic and endured many restrictions, which were all finally lifted on March 11, 2022.

---

[47] Tony Mballa, "Shigoli Surmounts Adversities to Foster Badminton in Kenya," *The Star*, July 30, 2022, https://www.the-star.co.ke/sports/2022-07-30-shigoli-surmounts-adversities-to-foster-badminton-in-kenya/.

Many of Sheila's hopes and dreams were put on hold because of COVID-19. Her work for an IT company, Cyber School Technology Solutions, which provides digital materials for secondary schools and transforms mathematics and science syllabuses into animations, was suspended. Her responsibilities had included selling the products throughout Kenya, making sure her team achieved daily targets, and training teachers to use the computers. All that ceased when the schools were closed, forcing her to find another source of income to make ends meet. She decided to focus on giving private badminton lessons at Jaffrey Sports Club and Aga Khan Sports Club, both in Nairobi.

"COVID-19 destabilised Kenya's economy since most businesses and institutions were shut down. It greatly affected me because my work dealt with schools, and they were closed. My coaching, too, was affected. First, sporting activities were suspended and, upon resumption, numbers were limited and some clients stopped their lessons because they feared COVID-19. It set the country, and me, back."

Rebuilding Her Future

Tenacious and ambitious, Sheila remains focused on developing her sport academy, but will first enrol in a sport management course, which she considers to be an important component of her goal to eventually vie for a position on the board of directors of Badminton Kenya, once its affairs are straightened out, and later with the NOCK. She is also optimistic about future employment in her chosen field, noting that universities are a regular source of sport management positions. Also, secondary schools with a sport department hire professionals to run their programmes.

She admits that, as a woman, she encounters challenges even though she is a certified international coach. That, she insists, should stand for something, but she notes, "It's mostly about people not believing in me. The male coaches have been in the industry for many years and I'm just starting. I also get inappropriate messages from some of my clients but have devised a way to deal with that."

Sheila continues to raise her son as a single mother. She lives with her sister, Jean, who works from home. Jean also has a child and so can tend to the children when they are not in school. A house helper, Lillian Achieng, is part of their household and lends a hand with childcare. "Griffin is used to me coming and going because of my coaching commitments, but I try my best to spend as much time with him as possible, especially keeping Sundays free for him."

Once Sheila's academy becomes a reality and once she locates an affordable venue, she intends to accommodate low-income families as well as the well-to-do who currently are most of her clients at the clubs. "I would like a future where I can have an impact through sport and, so far, it is going well. The NOCK and the International Olympic Committee are working to develop a stadium that can accommodate all sports, and I am hoping that, by the time it is completed, my academy can use it too."

Chapter Nineteen

Mpho Madi

South Africa

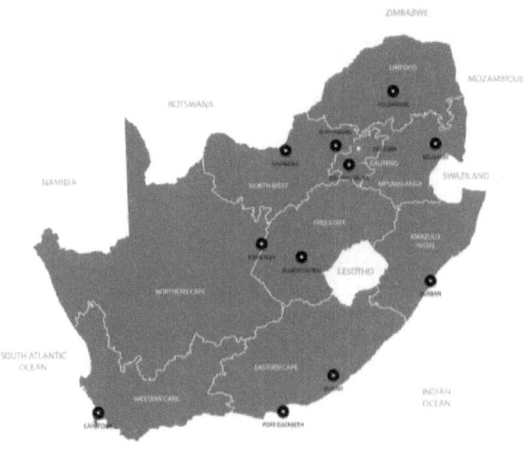

Mpho Madi is a fiercely independent champion athlete, university graduate, committed partner, loving mother, founder and president of a successful wrestling club, and aspiring leader of her sport. None of this was predictable.

Born on May 13, 1988, in Ermelo, Mpumalanga Province, South Africa, Mpho was immediately taken to a children's home, known generically as "a place of safety." She never knew her biological parents. "Their name was Skosana; that's all I know about them."

There she stayed until being adopted at the age of two by Philippine Madi, who had no children of her own, and Alfred Madi, who had six older children. "I need to talk about my early life so people can understand me."

Until Mpho was five, life was tolerable, but then Philippine began to mistreat her. Neighbours and friends, who suspected mental illness, called social services because they feared Mpho would die if not removed. For the next two years, Mpho moved from place to place because Philippine's relatives took her in when trouble erupted.

Instability was the norm until ten-year-old Mpho was placed at Kids Haven[48] in Benoni, Gauteng, just east of Johannesburg. Mpho would spend the rest of her growing-up years in Benoni. The town of about 94,000 began around 1887 as a mining camp after gold was discovered nearby. Today it's noted for mining, as well as some farming and other commercial enterprises.

As so often is the case in child abuse, Mpho accepted her situation as normal, not knowing any other way of being treated. However, once she arrived at Kids Haven, everything changed. "My life started when I got there. I started knowing what love is from a person. I had noticed kids being hugged by their parents, but I had never been hugged, and I thought that was how it was for me. I longed for love and family and friends who treated you well, and when I got to Kids Haven, I got all that."

The change was drastic. Suddenly Mpho had all the love she could want along with two hundred or so brothers and sisters. She started doing well academically and was introduced to the possibilities presented by sport — Kids Haven offered seventeen sports — and she grabbed every opportunity.

Soccer was the first sport at which she excelled, so much so that some suggested she could eventually play for the national team. When she was fourteen, a soccer friend, Siphiwe Sibiya, asked her to accompany him to practice at the Benoni Wrestling Club. As she sat watching, she asked coaches Hansie Naudé and Hannes Hietbrink if she could try it. "They agreed and I thought to myself, why not?" Not knowing a thing about wrestling, she defeated all the club members, prompting the coaches to insist that she return the following week

---

[48] Kids Haven (website), Kids Haven, accessed September 20, 2023, https://kidshaven.co.za/.

and enter her first competition one week later. "I said, 'Okay, thank you very much! Hansie taught me the basics from scratch, and they both made it easy to go back and want more."

In preparation for that first competition, Mpho trained for two days, and then wrestled and won at the trials to go to the National Junior Championships, where she won the 51 kg title. She was on her way.

For a while, Mpho continued to play soccer, not seeing a future in wrestling, and decided to go to the national soccer team trials. At the same time, her friend Mapule Segogela attended the national wrestling trials and won a spot on the junior national team and a trip to Turkey. Mpho was less fortunate; she missed making the soccer side. Knowing that she usually defeated her friend on the mat, she decided to switch to wrestling, drawn not only by the possibilities for travel, but because she loved to push herself and welcomed the challenges wrestling posed. "You challenge the people you wrestle with, but most importantly you challenge yourself. I pushed myself to the limit. I had to beat my opponents, even in training sessions, and I liked the discipline the sport requires. Also, when I saw my friend go to Turkey, nothing was going to stop me to also go overseas. If she can, why can't I? And wrestling was going to give me that opportunity."

A Stellar Athletic Career

Mpho made her international debut in 2007 when she competed at the All-Africa Games in Algiers, Algeria, and won the bronze medal. "It was my first time ever on an airplane and to go and represent my country, so it was a nice experience."

Next came the 2008 Junior World Championships in Istanbul, Turkey, where she placed ninth. "It was big, and I was so nervous, and there was war with fighting, bombs, and ambulances. So, not bad for a first comer."[49]

---

[49] On July 9, 2008, the Consulate General of the United States in Istanbul was attacked by three gunmen. The attackers and three Turkish national police officers were killed.

Mpho Madi speaking at the WCIP closing reception
Photographer: Murray Rix, Rix Ryan Photography Qld. Supplied by Griffith Uni Gold Coast, Queensland.

In 2009, at the age of twenty-one, Mpho left Kids Haven, where she'd met Amanda Van Der Watt, who had become the mother figure she had lacked and with whom she had lived when in Benoni. "Her granddaughter used to wrestle, and we got talking at a wrestling match. She supported me through the years until I started working."

Although Mpho's wrestling was progressing, the programme at Benoni Wrestling Club focused on the fundamentals and, when she decided she wanted more, that meant finding a club where the wrestlers were bigger and the training harder. And so, in 2009, she moved to the Boksburg Wrestling Club, located in Boksburg, a city on the East Rand of Gauteng Province and 10 kilometres from Benoni. There she came under the tutelage of Nico Coetzee, an internationally respected coach. He was junior national coach from 2006 and a senior national coach from 2009. His athletes won numerous medals at the Commonwealth Games, All-Africa Games, African Championships, and other international competitions.

"Nico was not just my coach; he was my father too. He used to say, 'Let's work hard now; you can rest after the competition.' And that meant I wouldn't rest until the Christmas holidays when competition stopped."

As Mpho's wrestling skills developed, she was also doing well academically. However, in 2007, a clash occurred between the World Junior Championships in Beijing, China, and the matriculation examinations that precede final examinations. "When I chose China (and finished twelfth) the school authorities agreed on the condition that I promise to work extra hard for the finals. I always passed exams without studying, but not this time. I failed three subjects, which meant I had to rewrite one year later. I stopped wrestling for six months and passed the exams with five distinctions!"

Mpho's next important competition was the 2010 Commonwealth Games in New Delhi, India, her first-ever Games. "I was really wowed about everything, from the moment we left the airport to arriving at the Athletes' Village. Seeing so many other athletes, free food, drinks, transportation, being able to watch other sports. Really, it was nice and I enjoyed it. Placing fourth inspired me to work harder for a medal in 2014 in Glasgow."

Even as Mpho's athletic and academic potential matured, she had no set goal, knowing only that, once she finished school, she would go to work. "I didn't want to go to university or be a professor or a doctor, I just wanted to work and make money; I love money!" Unexpectedly, she was awarded a bursary to study at Exercise Teachers Academy in Pretoria for a diploma to teach physical education. Upon graduation in 2011, at the age of twenty-three, she spent a year handling administration for Nico's home business (selling cleaning chemicals) and trying to figure out what to do with her life. Her days consisted of training each morning, teaching all day, and then more training.

South African women wrestlers were denied the opportunity to compete at the 2012 Olympic Games in London, England, after Nico declared that they were "not fit to even try to qualify." Mpho decided to take a one-year child psychology course at the University of Pretoria. It took only one semester for her to realise that it was not for her, but she stayed to graduate, being committed to finishing whatever she started. Once done, she concentrated on training for the 2014 Commonwealth Games in Glasgow, Scotland, living either with Esta Van Zyl, the coach of the national women's team, or Nico and his wife, Debbie, who were always key figures in her life. "Their presence helped me close the gap of not growing up with parents."

Mpho made South Africa's team at the trials held in conjunction with the 2013 Commonwealth Championships in Johannesburg, which she described as "the most difficult competition of [her] life." In her weight class of 53 kg, she was up against stiff competition. However, buoyed by the home crowd and in the best shape of her life, she earned her spot with a strong second-place finish. "Going to those trials, I was focused. I knew what I wanted. I would leave the wow-wows until the end of the competition. It was a different mindset [from 2010] and I was ready."

Thirty Seconds and the Bronze Medal

"I lost my first match. I was so excited that I forgot my wrestling shoes. I had to wrestle with my friend's shoes, and they were slightly too big so not comfortable at all. If I had won that match, I might have wrestled in the final, but I had to wrestle three matches before wrestling for the bronze medal. It was a first for South African wrestling.

"I was wrestling a Scottish girl, Shannon Hawke. Imagine wrestling a Scottish girl in Scotland. I didn't eat lunch because I didn't want to overeat. Nico stayed with me and kept telling me I was going to win; I had a long two hours to wait. My body told me I was ready for the match. I wasn't scared, I wasn't shy, but when I saw the TV crew from South Africa, I started shaking.

"I used to ask Nico to pat me a little so my nerves would vanish. I didn't ask him this time, but he did it anyway. Shannon walked in first, and the crowd went wild. When I walked in it was so quiet, I could hear my footsteps. My friend yelled, 'You go!' I thought to myself, I'm going to finish this very quickly. I wrestled thirty seconds, and I pinned her. Winning that medal was life-changing for a child with no parents; when I saw where my life was, I was proud."

Winning that bronze medal did change Mpho's life. For one thing, she met President Jacob Zuma and Minister of Sport and Recreation Fikile Mbalula. Even better, two months after Glasgow, she flew to Busan, South Korea, having been awarded a one-year bursary to study at Dong-A University, the only South African wrestler so honoured. Her academic programme — international sports relations combined with Korean culture and an internship focused on the organisation of the upcoming 2018 Winter Olympic Games in PyeongChang — was designed to provide retired or retiring athletes with the skills, experience, and advice needed to successfully transition from sport. Mpho remembers her time in Busan as her best study years. When a friend wondered how she, as an English speaker, would manage in an Asian country, she replied: "I've been through a lot in life; why not this?" She was proud of her ability to take the train from Seoul to Busan without having to ask anyone for help. "There was little information in English, but I did very well!"

Mpho relished the independence afforded by life in Busan and enjoyed pushing herself through her gruelling schedule. Classes ran from 9:00 a.m. to 11:30 p.m., with breaks and time off for lunch and dinner. Her schedule left little time for training, and she decided to retire from wrestling. Nico agreed, saying she had nothing left to prove. Studies completed, Mpho was offered a job teaching English to older people on Jeju Island, South Korea's largest and most populous island. "I loved being in another country but didn't want to be so far away from my people." She returned to Johannesburg in 2016 to work as a physical education teacher at Helpmekaar College, a private Afrikaans college where she also coached wrestling.

Transition Time

Mpho started coaching in 2009, working with youngsters at the Boksburg Wrestling Club. From then on, she took provincial coach education courses and achieved National Level 5, which allowed her to coach at international events. She taught and coached at the college until 2018, when she was selected to take part in the WCIP. Nico had told her about the programme and, not surprisingly, she quickly applied. "I enjoyed everything about the WCIP experience. It was interesting that we all had a similar story to tell: You are a woman coach and people don't really take you seriously ... [WCIP] opened another window for me as a woman coach ... Women in coaching will grow because I share my learnings."

Inspired by the WCIP experience, Mpho was determined to start her own wrestling club. Moving quickly, she decided to locate her club, which she named the Battleground Wrestling Club, in the disadvantaged township of Tsakane, Brakpan. She was intent on teaching life skills as well as wrestling and getting youngsters off the streets and into the training room.

Provided with two wrestling mats and a government hall, in 2019 Mpho advertised a wrestling clinic in local newspapers and on television. She was shocked when five hundred youngsters indicated their interest; her expectation had been twenty or so. Ever resourceful, she moved the clinic from the hall to a rugby field where, assisted by her training partners, she demonstrated the fundamentals of the sport to the two hundred who turned up. It was a promising start, and the novice wrestlers quickly began to win competitions. Before long, Mpho secured the financial support of the National Lotteries Commission, which continues. Initially the head coach and currently the club's president, she now has forty-five registered wrestlers, two team managers, and five registered coaches who have achieved Provincial Level 3 coaching certification, meaning they are eligible to coach at national championships.

Also in 2019, United World Wrestling, her international body, invited Mpho to be part of the organising committee for the African Championships in Hammamet, Tunisia, and to work with its development department as assistant to the technical director. She delivered the International Olympic Committee Athlete Learning Gateway to wrestlers in Tunisia and coached the South African team at the 2019 Cadet World Championships, the first woman coach to ever attend the event. "Thank you, WCIP!"

COVID-19 Causes Interruptions

South Africa's first patient was confirmed on March 5, 2020, and the country experienced several waves between then and April 4, 2022. On March 15, 2020, President Cyril Ramaphosa declared a national state of disaster, prohibiting gatherings of more than one hundred people. On March 18, the government limited the number of patrons at pubs, clubs, and restaurants to fifty. Parliament suspended all activities, and schools were closed, with resumption planned for early June. Most universities suspended classes around this time as well.

The state of disaster was extended to September 15 and lasted for almost two more years, until midnight on April 4, 2022, when the national state of disaster ended, though some transitional provisions remained in place for another thirty days.

Given the situation, Mpho had no choice but to close Battleground Wrestling Club. The young wrestlers were kept busy by programmes she devised and through a WhatsApp group she established so they could send her videos of their activities. She was able to sit out the closure because her partner, Vincent Aka, the regional officer of Africa Wrestling, was earning enough money to keep their household going. Vincent, also a wrestler and from the Ivory Coast, represented his home country at the 2000 Olympic Games and, after obtaining French citizenship, competed for France at the 2004 and 2008 Olympic Games.

Battleground reopened in January 2022 and has flourished ever since. Twelve of its wrestlers are national champions; four are women and eight are men.

Growing Responsibilities

During the pandemic, Mpho became pregnant with twins. Her daughter, Onthatile Adjoua Madi, and son, Thato Kouadio Madi, were born on October 27, 2020. She notes with a laugh that her wrestlers didn't believe she had children, because they never saw her during the pregnancy. She was well for most of the time but fell ill two weeks before the birth and had to have a caesarean at thirty-seven weeks. After a three-day stay in hospital, curtailed because space was required for COVID patients, she returned home.

With much sadness, Mpho learned that Nico died suddenly of a heart attack at the age of fifty-six on May 25, 2021. It was some consolation that he had met the babies, having visited Mpho on February 27, 2021. She treasures photos of the visit.

Mpho's activism dates to 2017 when she was elected as the first female vice president of the Eastern Gauteng Wrestling Association, the first Black woman to serve as an executive of a provincial sport body in South Africa. Her goal is to "bring women's wrestling alive in South Africa by developing and grooming young women to become coaches, officials, team managers, and board members."

A personal goal she described as "realistic" is to one day become president of the South African Wrestling Federation. "Others are also interested, but nowadays, in a democratic South Africa, if an organisation requests a government subsidy, certain questions are asked. How many Black people are in your sport? How many women? How many Black women? All of that counts for me."

While Mpho agreed that she is benefitting from the dismantling of apartheid in South Africa, she explained that she was never affected by the racial segregation that dictated that non-white South Africans live in separate areas from white people and use separate public facilities. "I ask people what it was like because I grew up with a lot of white people, including at Kids Haven. In wrestling and as a teacher, I am around a lot of white people who have always been friendly and nice to me."

Recognition

Mpho's coaching has brought her recognition in the form of numerous awards, including club, provincial, national, and Protea colours (national colours) from 2006 to 2016. She was Ekurhuleni Sportswoman of the Year in 2007 and 2015; Club Sportswoman of the Year from 2006 to

2016; Eastern Province Sportswoman of the Year from 2009 to 2015; and a finalist for the South Africa Sport Award in 2014.

Mpho Madi's wrestling club is thriving post-pandemic.

As her children grow, Mpho is pleased that both love to wrestle, although she has no intention of coaching them. "I might be too harsh or too soft, so I'd rather someone else coach them. I think they must be sporty little ones, although my boy likes to sing and read, and my girl is jollier and more playful. I can't wait to see how they develop."

Happily, Mpho and her adoptive parents reconciled in 2014, and when they passed away, they left her a house in a suburb of Benoni called Crystal Park, where she and her family live. She also invited her adoptive mother's nephew and his daughter to live there. "I like them, and I help where I can. And yes, I forgave my adoptive parents, and now the Madi family is part of my life."

Whatever Mpho's future holds, coaching will be at the heart of everything she does. "I am no longer teaching; I'm coaching and loving it. Listen! Coaching is my life. When I go to the club, I'm not just a coach, I'm also a mother to those kids. That changes the whole perspective of coaching. I travel an hour each way to get from Benoni to the club in Boksburg. I am determined that my wrestlers make something of themselves out of wrestling."

Chapter Twenty

Evangeline Collier

England

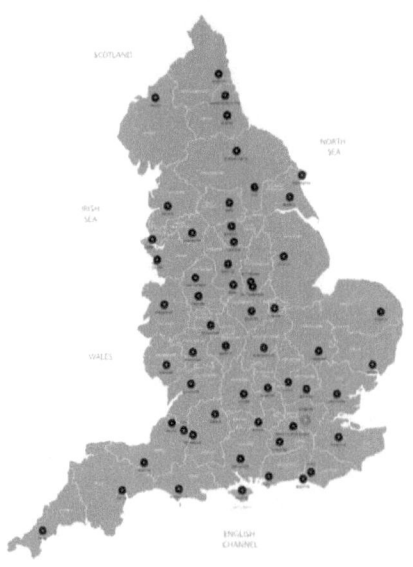

Evangeline (Evie) Collier's life has revolved around table tennis since she was seven years old, and her passion for the sport shows no signs of abating. Combining years of playing and coaching and carrying a heavy scholastic load, excellence has characterised all her endeavours.

Evie was born in Chelmsford, Essex, on September 16, 1994, to Paul, an insurance broker, and Sherlayne, a learning support assistant. Shortly afterwards, the family settled in Brentwood, a suburban town in the county of Essex where Sherlayne was born. Sports of all kinds and plenty of outdoor activity characterised Evie's childhood. She excelled at running and loved swimming, football, and netball — anything that kept her active — but she was intrigued by the speed of table tennis and with the angles created when playing the shots and where you could get the ball to bounce on the table by changing the angles slightly.

Fortuitously, Evie's primary school offered its students table tennis, an uncommon option made possible by Nick Jarvis, a teacher and a former international player for England. Even at the age of seven, Evie loved playing and quickly took to the training regime devised by Jarvis.

By the age of nine, students were expected to decide whether to carry on with table tennis or switch to other sports. Evie chose to balance table tennis with cross country running until she was fifteen, when it had to be one or the other, and table tennis won out. Jarvis' coaching played a major role in her choice. "His style is straightforward and nurturing. I am a determined individual and a perfectionist, and, from a young age, I would get frustrated if I didn't achieve a goal. He knew how to get the best out of me and gave up a lot of time to help me. He taught me how to push myself without relying on other people. I owe a lot to him for being there in my first ten years or so of table tennis."

"I fell in love with table tennis as soon as I picked the bat up, and twenty-two years on, the love affair continues. I'm naturally competitive and wanted to be the best ... As the years went on, I loved the dimensions of competition training, learning new spins, and of course winning matches."

Family, including her sisters Grace and Lucie, was another factor in enabling Evie to fulfil her dream of international play. "They gave up a lot of family time taking me to competitions at home and abroad. They gave up a lot for me to do what I love."

By the age of seventeen, Evie was the top-ranked female player in the county, her potential undeniable. She won the silver medal after being called up to play for England at Senior Schools International in Guernsey; placed third at the School National Individual Championships; won the singles title at the Hasselt International Youth Cup in Belgium; was the 2012 Essex Young Sports Personality of the Year; was presented with the Player of the Year award by head coach and England International Alex Perry; and was signed by Belgium Team Dienst, one of that country's leading table tennis clubs.

"During college, I was out for four months with a broken foot, but that didn't stop me. I focused heavily on gym work and trained sitting in a chair to continue to develop my feeling for the ball. If anything, this sparked my determination to come back better and stronger. I never let things like that hold me back; they made me strive even more to be the best."

In 2011, at the age of eighteen, Evie moved north to Grantham, a market and industrial town in Lincolnshire, to attend Grantham College Table Tennis Academy, recognised countrywide as a leading place for young players to train and study. "I wanted to be the best table tennis player I could and so I didn't hesitate in going to Grantham."

Evie Collier speaking at the WCIP closing reception
Photographer: Murray Rix, Rix Ryan Photography Qld. Supplied by Griffith Uni Gold Coast, Queensland.

Building a High Performance Resume

In 2013, Evie moved again, this time to the East Midlands city of Nottingham, famous for its links to the legend of Robin Hood. It's also known for lace-making, bicycle, and tobacco industries, and for being a thriving table tennis centre. Awarded a scholarship because of her ranking in England, success abroad, and top grades, Evie enrolled at Nottingham Trent University (NTU) to study for a bachelor of arts degree in sport education and special, inclusive education. Her research focused on how universities promote female sports and use female sporting initiatives to encourage participation in sport and physical activity.

Choosing NTU made sense because, according to its website, NTU has "the strongest and most established table tennis programme of any UK university, with an impressive history of national and international triumphs ... Its sports village acts as a hub for English performance table tennis, hosts England national squad training, and provides NTU students with access to regular training and coaching alongside the world's top 100 players. Strong links to China, Malaysia, and Europe also offer NTU players the opportunity to compete and train abroad."[50]

Evie enjoyed stellar results during her undergraduate years. She won a BUCS (British Universities & Colleges Sport) national trophy and the BUCS Midlands 1A league, the highest level of university table tennis. She then represented Great Britain at the 2015 World University Games in Gwangju, South Korea. "As a player this experience will forever be in my head. Even now, the feel of the arena, wearing my Great Britain kit, it brings back a familiar sense of gratitude. I lost to a player ranked in the top thirty in the world. It was a real pinch-me moment, being in a major Games environment."

In 2017, Evie completed her master of arts focusing on special education and inclusive education with an emphasis on physical activity. "I've always had a passion for helping kids with disabilities.

---

[50] "About NTU," Nottingham Trent University, accessed September 20, 2023, https://www.ntu.ac.uk/about-us, https://www.ntu.ac.uk/sport/clubs/table-tennis.

For my thesis, I examined how physical activity can help children with special needs, mainly attention deficit disorder, with both their academic achievement levels and their engagement in lessons. NTU was fantastic. I was awarded an additional scholarship for academic excellence, and they supported me with extensions when I needed to compete. I had a great support team, especially during periods of stress. I absolutely loved my time at university."

Earning her master's was a point of pride for Evie. "It was a tough year with a lot of learning. It was my first proper year of coaching. I was still playing and coaching. I was learning to balance everything, and it was a struggle. Coming out on top was the best thing. I got through it!"

Coaching Came Naturally

Evie's involvement with the Carlton le Willows Academy in Nottingham from 2017 to 2019 piqued her interest in becoming a high performance table tennis coach. It was an ideal situation because she was able to both train and coach. First as a learning mentor and then as a learning hub coordinator, she worked with youngsters with additional needs and those who struggled to learn within the traditional learning/classroom environment. "I got to play the sport I love, I got to coach the sport I love, and hopefully I was able to support pupils to achieve what they thought wasn't possible."

Keen to encourage girls to play table tennis, Evie stressed the importance of girls having women role models during their growing-up years. She noted that women coaches often encounter stereotypes about their ability to coach. From her experience, while acknowledging that she has benefitted from excellent male coaches, Evie noticed that girls tend to be "more relaxed knowing there is a woman they can talk to if something is bothering them. Most women coaches have an empathetic and sympathetic approach and may be less judgemental."

Evie Collier enjoys coaching young, talented players.

As Evie's interest in coaching grew, she began to accumulate coach education credits. However, as a hands-on person, working at training camps and competitions alongside experienced coaches has been at least as beneficial to progressing her career. Before long, she was given her first assignment coaching for England, taking a squad to a female Cadet competition in June 2017 in the Netherlands. This was followed by coaching the Cadet girls at the European Six Nations event in July in Germany, the season's biggest tournament. "I was still very much a player, but now I saw such a dimension of table tennis I had never seen before ... Nick [Jarvis] always said I would be involved in the coaching side, and he was right."

WCIP: A Major Turning Point

As the 2018 Commonwealth Games in Gold Coast, Australia, approached, Evie was still relatively new to coaching with Table

Tennis England (TTE) — she became a national coach in 2017, having started on a camp-by-camp basis one year earlier — and was hoping to play for Team England.

When Simon Mills, the TTE performance director, was notified that the Commonwealth Games Federation would be running a Women Coach Internship Programme throughout the Games, he contacted Evie to ask if she was interested in applying. Although focused more on playing than coaching at the time, Evie immediately said yes after reading the application form. Acceptance into the WCIP, which included the position of assistant coach of Team England and mentorship with Alan Cooke, then the head coach of Great Britain and England, proved to be critical to her steady progression as a coach.

Evie, who is slow to trust people and open up in new situations, didn't know what to expect as she nervously entered the meeting room for the first WCIP session. "I'll never forget that day. When something is new and I'm thousands of miles from home in a place I have never been before and coming into a roomful of fantastic coaches and not knowing anyone, I was very, very scared and shy and lacking in confidence. As soon as Sheilagh and Sheila[51] spoke, I felt a complete weight fall off my shoulders and I thought, This is amazing. I want to grab the opportunity with both hands.

"From the first, it was as though I had known the other coaches for ages. And I was so engaged at the table tennis hall, soaking up everything. I walked around with a big grin on my face!"

A prime purpose of the WCIP was to embed the intern coaches with their teams on the field of play, thereby assuring that they would experience the Games fully and have an opportunity to showcase their coaching skills, laying the groundwork for further coaching opportunities upon returning home. Evie's Games-time and post-Games experiences, which have been, in large part, shared by her

---

[51] Sheilagh Croxon, a former Olympic coach, designed, implemented, and led the WCIP session. Sheila Hurtig Robertson, an author and editor of the *Canadian Journal for Women in Coaching* (https://coach.ca/canadian-journal-women-coaching), was the programme's communications consultant.

fellow interns, demonstrated the success that WCIP was and continues to be.

Evie credited the WCIP for developing her confidence to seek additional coaching opportunities within England with development camps, and abroad. For example, she was head coach of the Cadet girls' team at the 2019 European Youth Championships in Ostrava, Czech Republic, the only woman of four coaches, and said this was "such a big learning experience." Earlier, at the 2018 International Table Tennis Federation Team World Cup, she was assigned various responsibilities as part of the coaching staff and also trained with the female athletes, all of which gave her big-event experience. She led a development programme at the Nottingham Table Tennis Club. She attended several tournaments, both in a support and coaching capacity, with England and the UK and served as lead on several trips across Europe and all around the world, including South Korea, Peru, and Brazil. She has frequently been the female point of contact for these teams and, while she supported all players, she ensured that the women had access to the competitions they needed to develop.

"I was in awe of everything; I felt like a sponge. I was taking in so much information; every day was amazing and inspiring. It became the big stepping stone in my development and showing me what I want to get out of being a coach and inspiring the next generation of women players and coaches."

Evie's experience in Gold Coast was enhanced by the mentoring and guidance of the English coaches with whom she worked, especially Alan Cooke. "The mentoring has developed me so much as a coach. Most days Alan would sit down with me, and I could ask him questions … he gave up a lot of time for my questions. To him, no question was silly. I want to be a coach like that, approachable and supportive, to have players come to me with questions or if they're struggling."

Evie has also been inspired to keep progressing as a coach by the WCIP network that continues through WhatsApp and personal exchanges. "It's so supportive to have such a group to talk to. If I'm struggling, I can reach out to them and be inspired by their support. We understand each other's struggles."

COVID-19 Strikes Hard and Fast

In the United Kingdom, the pandemic resulted in nearly 25 million confirmed cases and is associated with more than 200,000 deaths. Nationwide restrictions, including lockdowns, were introduced to mitigate the impact, and economic support was given to struggling businesses, including a furlough scheme for employees. The pandemic disrupted education and impacted the economy, society, politics, and sport. As Evie noted, "Sport was massively impacted. I went from working out and training every day to everything being online as sports clubs and gyms were all closed down. And we were only allowed outside once a day!"

As a player, the pandemic meant Evie was unable to practise or compete for the longest period of her career, and for a few weeks, having a rest was welcomed. But once the pleasures of the respite wore off, coping with the situation became difficult. "I did struggle. At first, working out and running was my release, but then we entered lockdown and for about three weeks, I couldn't do either."

As a coach, Evie and her fellow coaches gradually adapted, using Zoom to communicate with their players and leading web sessions on a wide variety of topics. "We learned what we needed to do to keep them in shape physically so that when we returned to the hall in September 2022, we could focus on technique. It was great to be back and doing the sport I love, so I was incredibly happy."

One positive result of the lockdowns was an enhanced love for playing the sport. Evie happily prepared for the upcoming competitive season, which included playing for Young Stars Zurich in Switzerland, a team she had played with for three years. "I had a lovely balance between playing and coaching. I'm a structured, organised person — some might think I am crazy busy — but I try to tailor everything, so I get the most out of both."

Change and a Bright Future

The end of the pandemic brought a major change as Evie left teaching to accept the position of administration and logistics officer with the

TTE. Her responsibilities include working with the Great Britain Table Tennis Committee and the Table Tennis England Talent and Performance Committee. She also retired from playing. "I have found a true purpose in my role of supporting our athletes. I support athletes both within the competition environment and on the operational side, including all bookings, transfers, accommodation, and meals. I always jump on the table when our young talented players are in camp. I feel a real sense of supporting them as they start their table tennis journey. I believe in giving back and supporting the future generations."

Evie welcomes the opportunities she now has to work alongside many experienced coaches, such as Gavin Evans and Ryan Jenkins, with their own individual stories and experiences. "Table tennis is a very skill-specific sport, and working every day with Gavin and Ryan and other members of our team is to really provide our athletes with the support to reach their potential."

Although Evie wishes for more women table tennis coaches as colleagues, she knows that the barriers she has faced are not as insurmountable as elsewhere. TTE has provided education and support. "Whatever I've needed, they've made sure I had. It's tough being a woman coach, but the support I've had has made it easier. And the support must continue. So many of us drop out of the sport, and it is vital to provide them with avenues to continue. It's such a male-dominated sport, and now I am part of a great team with a goal of supporting women coaches and players."

Evie has a passion for travel, and her position with TTE offers her many opportunities to explore far and wide as she travels to training camps and tournaments. She is determined to squeeze everything possible out of life, combining experiences with self-development. Having secured her dream job within the sport she loves, she has new goals that include working towards programme manager roles, working on the operational side of major Games, coaching the national women's team, and serving as team lead for Team England at the Commonwealth Games or Team GB at the Olympic Games.

Evie's coaching is focused primarily on the younger players, and she supports Kelly Sibley who leads the TTE's Futures programme.

Along with Nicola Deaton, they round out the Futures coaching team. TTE emerged from recent restructuring with a relatively new and young team Evie describes as "a power ball. We all have a focus on developing table tennis and becoming world-class players, coaches, and the team as a whole.

"My life goal is based around table tennis and the coaching element. The more I'm enjoying coaching, the more opportunities I'm getting as my coaching goes from strength to strength. The pandemic gave me the opportunity to think about how far I've come, professionally and personally, and I will always be thankful for the fantastic WCIP coaches.

"'The unbreakable bond' is not too strong a phrase to describe the WCIP experience. It is hard to explain the bonds we have. It is almost like a sisterhood of amazing women coaches who are taking the world by storm in terms of inspiring athletes and each other. It's a massive bond that I imagine is hard for people to understand, a bond of women from around the world, different sports, different ages, different life experiences, but we were brought together, and it was like a fireball of knowledge and experience. I don't think the bond will ever be broken."

Appendix One:

CGF Women Coach Internship Programme Application Form

Proposed Candidate / Sponsoring Organizations

Please provide the following information.

Candidate Name	
Candidate Email and telephone number Sport (and event if applicable)	
CGA:	
CGA Contact Name and position CGA Email and telephone number	
National Sport Organization (NSO)	

NSO Contact Name and position NSO Email and telephone number	
Mentor Coach Name Mentor Coach Email and telephone number	

Candidate Qualifications

Please provide information on the candidate's previous coaching experience and the relevance of this opportunity for their future progression as a coach. Please submit a resume for the candidate with this application.

Training / Certifications: (include dates where applicable)	
Community, Regional, or National Coaching Experience:	
WCIP contribution to their Individual's Coaching Career post-Games:	

Team Role / Support

The candidate, if selected, is expected to fulfil a specific and meaningful role within the coaching team and on the field of play. An appropriate support environment for the intern coach is expected so the intern can obtain a meaningful experience within a coaching team at a multisport Game.

A Games-time mentor coach must be assigned to each intern coach. The mentor coach must be a member of the Games' coaching staff. The intern coach must also have a point of contact within the Team's management team for non-coaching related support. Every attempt must be made to ensure the best possible Games-time mentor coach is selected for the intern coach. Please submit a resume for the Games-time mentor coach with this application.

Role the intern coach will play at Games-time:	

Games-time Coach Mentor Background and Experience:	

Proposed support and mentorship model for the intern coach at Games-time:	

Post-Games Support

Post-Games support for the intern coach within their sport is critical for the ongoing success of the candidate and the WCIP. Please describe how the CGA and NSO will support the intern coach to progress her coaching career in-country upon her return.

Post-Games In-country Support Model:	

Approvals

Through signature below, the following organizations / individuals agree to submit this application and in doing so, agree to support the nominated intern coach and to deliver the expected commitments as outlined in the WCIP Programme Guidelines

Date Submitted:	
Candidate:	
CGA:	
National Sport Organization (NSO):	
Mentor Coach:	

Appendix Two:
CGF Women Coach Internship Programme Guidelines

Post-Games Evaluation

At the completion of the 2018 Commonwealth Games, the WCIP will be evaluated against desired outcomes.

The post-Games evaluation will involve CGAs/NSOs, Games-time mentor coaches, and intern coaches. Each will be expected to complete a feedback survey in order to provide constructive suggestions for improvements for the future iterations of the WCIP. As well, interviews with some or all participants will be undertaken.

Evaluation results will help fine-tune post Games mentorship, support, and networking aspects of the WCIP as well as the design of future iterations.

Timelines

The timelines for the application and decision are as follows:
- Application Guideline and Form Issued: August 15, 2017
- Applications Due Date: September 30, 2017
- Adjudication and determination of eligibility: October 2017
- Notification of successful candidates: October 31, 2017
- Intern Coach introductory call: December 2017

- Professional Development programme: January and February 2018 (need to provide detail on the commitment required during this period)
- Gold Coast Games: April 4–15, 2018

The CGF Director of Sport will screen applications against the eligibility and selection criteria. Each application meeting basic expectations will be forwarded to the Sport Committee for review and decision.

Completed application forms are to be submitted by September 2012.

Appendix Three:

Women Coach Internship Programme

Programme Schedule

All sessions will be held in the Commonwealth Games Village
Thursday, 5th April, 2018
7:30-9:00 a.m. WCIP Introductory Session *Presented by Sheilagh Croxon* Followed by Group Photo
Friday, 6th April, 2018
7:30-8:15 a.m. Morning Message 8:15-8:30 Walk to Griffith University 8:30-9:30 a.m. Sport Science Made Easy *Presented by Assistant Professor Clare Minahan, Griffith University*
Saturday, 7th April, 2018
7:30-8:30 a.m. Morning Message

8:30-10:00 a.m. 'From the Field' Stories and Advice from Women Coaches *Presented by Anastasia Umeh and Joan Smit*

Sunday, 8th April, 2018
8-8:30 a.m. Morning Message 8:30-10:00 a.m. MBTI Assessment *Presented by Dr. Claire Carver-Dias* 1:00-2:00 p.m. Understanding the International Sport System *Presented by David Grevemberg CEO CGF*

Monday, 9th April, 2018
7:30-8:30 a.m. Morning Message 8:30-9:00 Walk to Coaches House 9:00-10:00 a.m. Coaches House Keynote *Presented by Sir Graham Henry, High Performance Consultant and Former All Blacks Head Coach* 1:00-2:00 p.m. Coaches House Keynote *Presented by Alyson Annan Head Coach, Women's Hockey Team | Netherlands*

Tuesday, 10th April, 2018
7:30-8:00 a.m. Morning Message 8-8:30 a.m. 'From the Field' *Presented by Aisha Norvil, Swimming Team Barbados*

8:30-9:30 a.m. Media Do's and Don'ts *Presented by Sheila Robertson*

Wednesday, 11th April, 2018

7:30-8:30 a.m. Morning Message 8:30-:00 Walk to Coaches House 9:00-10:00 a.m. Coaches House Keynote — National Leadership & Games Coaching *Presented by John Atkinson, National Performance Director, Swimming Canada* 1:00-2:00 p.m. Coaches House HP Coach Panel Discussion — Coaches as Mentors and Leaders *Presented by Peggy Liddick (Gymnastics), Tracey Menzies (Swimming), Ellen Randall (Rowing), Iryna Dvoskina (Para and Able- Bodied Athletics), and Pauline Harrison (Moderator)*

Thursday, 12th April, 2018

7:30-8:30 a.m. Morning Message 8:30-9:30 a.m. Mentoring Women Coaches (For WCIP Mentors) *Presented by Sheilagh Croxon* 2:00-3:00 p.m. Coaches House — Women Leaders in Sport Panel Discussion 3:00-5:00 p.m. Women Coaches Reception *Hosted by Commonwealth Games Federation and Australian Institute of Sport*

Friday, 13th April, 2018

7:30-9:00 a.m. Navigating the way forward for continuing your development

Presented by Dr Sue Whatman, Griffith University 8:30-10:00 a.m. 'From the Field' Stories and Advice from Women Coaches *Presented by Glynis Nunn OAM — Gold Coast Academy of Sport*
Saturday, 14th April, 2018
7:30-9:00 a.m. WCIP Closing Session *Presented by Sheilagh Croxon* *This programme is supported in partnership by AIS, ICCE, Griffith University, and Commonwealth Games Australia.*

Appendix Four:

The WCIP Intern Coaches and Their Mentor Coaches

Amanda Booth and Grant Robbins

Dumisani Chauke and Norma Plummer

Evangeline Collier and Alan Cooke

Martine Dugrenier and Tonya Verbeek

Sheila Gakii and John Odhiambo

Mildred Gamba and Nalis Bigingo

Victoria Grant and Stu Ross

Tina Hoeben and Martyn Wilby

Lini Kazim and Peter Lau

Laura Kerr Lewis and Jackie Newton

Carolyne Anyango Kola and John Anzrah

Isabelle Lindor-André and Patrick Sahajasein

Mpho Madi and Nico Coetzee

Bah Chui Mei and Zuraidi Puteh

Grace Mmolai and Luza Lechedzani

Amanda Murphy and Dale Stevenson

Cordelia Norris and Steve Gladding

Endurance Ojokolo and Olu Sule

Jill Perry and Daniel Trépanier

Soraya Julaya Santos and Orlando Dingne

www.ingramcontent.com/pod-product-compliance
Lightning Source LLC
Chambersburg PA
CBHW020327170426
43200CB00006B/302